Lars Jäger

Handbook of ░░░ s
Compoun░ ░A)

F░

Frankfurt 2021

Lars Jäger

Handbook of Uniform Series Compound Amount (USCA) Factors

International Edition

Frankfurt 2021

Impressum / Imprint

Bibliografische Information der Deutschen Nationalbibliothek:
Die Deutsche Nationalbibliothek verzeichnet diese Publikation in der Deutschen Nationalbibliografie; detaillierte bibliografische Daten sind im Internet über http://dnb.dnb.de abrufbar.

© 2021 by Prof. Dr. Lars Jäger

Production and publishing: BoD – Books on Demand, Norderstedt, Germany.

ISBN: 9783753436166

PREFACE

This handbook contains uniform series compound amount (USCA) factors for negative and positive interest rates. Due to the development at the international financial markets negative interest rates are relevant for the valuation of investments. This book offers you a very simple, quick and effective way to calculate the future value of a uniform series of payments (payment in arrears). Therefore it uses the ‚factor method´. Learn to use the method in some minutes. It´s so easy! Just multiply the uniform cash flow with the USCA factor. That´s all.

Frankfurt, May 2021   Prof. Dr. Lars Jäger

The future value (FV) of uniform payment series

The future value of a uniform payment series (payment in arrears) is the result of compounding the interest (i) over a specific time (n years). Possible taxes or friction costs are ignored! In the following tables you will find the uniform series compound amount (USCA) factors.

The USCA factors based on the calculation for one payment unit (1 $). For the calculation of the future value of a concret uniform series you have just to multiply the USCA factor with the uniform cash flow.

USCA-factor equation:

$$USCA = \frac{(1+i)^n - 1}{(1+i) - 1}$$

How to find the USCA-Factor in the tables

You just have to search for the interest rate you like to use for compounding (column in the table) and the number of years (rows).

i	2.00	2.05
Years		
1	1.00000000	1.00000000
2	2.02000000	2.02050000
3	3.06040000	3.06192025
4	4.12160800	4.12468962
5	5.20404016	5.20924575
6	6.30812096	6.31603529
7	7.43428338	7.44551401
8	8.58296905	8.59814705
9	9.75462843	9.77440907
10	10.94972100	10.97478445
11	12.16871542	12.19976753
12	13.41208973	13.44986277

Future value calculation with USCA-factors

Example:
We search the future value (FV) of a uniform series of annual cash flows of 10,000 $ over 10 years (payment in arrears). The interest rate is 2 percent.

In this case, the annual cash flow of 10,000 $ has to be multiplied with the USCA factor of 10.94972100 (see table). The future value is 109,497.21 $.

Uniform Series Compound Amount (USCA) Factors

for negative interest rates

i	-1.50	-1.45	-1.40	-1.35	-1.30
Years					
1	1.00000000	1.00000000	1.00000000	1.00000000	1.00000000
2	1.98500000	1.98550000	1.98600000	1.98650000	1.98700000
3	2.95522500	2.95671025	2.95819600	2.95968225	2.96116900
4	3.91089663	3.91383795	3.91678126	3.91972654	3.92267380
5	4.85223318	4.85708730	4.86194632	4.86681023	4.87167904
6	5.77944968	5.78665954	5.79387907	5.80110829	5.80834722
7	6.69275793	6.70275297	6.71276476	6.72279333	6.73283870
8	7.59236656	7.60556305	7.61878606	7.63203562	7.64531180
9	8.47848107	8.49528239	8.51212305	8.52900314	8.54592275
10	9.35130385	9.37210079	9.39295333	9.41386160	9.43482575
11	10.21103429	10.23620533	10.26145198	10.28677447	10.31217302
12	11.05786878	11.08778036	11.11779165	11.14790301	11.17811477
13	11.89200075	11.92700754	11.96214257	11.99740632	12.03279927
14	12.71362073	12.75406593	12.79467258	12.83544134	12.87637288
15	13.52291642	13.56913198	13.61554716	13.66216288	13.70898004
16	14.32007268	14.37237956	14.42492950	14.47772368	14.53076330
17	15.10527159	15.16398006	15.22298049	15.28227441	15.34186337
18	15.87869251	15.94410235	16.00985876	16.07596370	16.14241915
19	16.64051213	16.71291286	16.78572074	16.85893819	16.93256770
20	17.39090444	17.47057563	17.55072065	17.63134253	17.71244432
21	18.13004088	18.21725228	18.30501056	18.39331940	18.48218254
22	18.85809026	18.95310212	19.04874041	19.14500959	19.24191417
23	19.57521891	19.67828214	19.78205804	19.88655196	19.99176929
24	20.28159063	20.39294705	20.50510923	20.61808351	20.73187629
25	20.97736677	21.09724932	21.21803770	21.33973938	21.46236189
26	21.66270627	21.79133920	21.92098517	22.05165290	22.18335119
27	22.33776567	22.47536478	22.61409138	22.75395559	22.89496762
28	23.00269919	23.14947200	23.29749410	23.44677719	23.59733304
29	23.65765870	23.81380465	23.97132918	24.13024570	24.29056772
30	24.30279382	24.46850448	24.63573058	24.80448738	24.97479033
31	24.93825191	25.11371117	25.29083035	25.46962680	25.65011806
32	25.56417813	25.74956236	25.93675872	26.12578684	26.31666653
33	26.18071546	26.37619370	26.57364410	26.77308872	26.97454986
34	26.78800473	26.99373889	27.20161308	27.41165202	27.62388071
35	27.38618466	27.60232968	27.82079050	28.04159472	28.26477026
36	27.97539189	28.20209590	28.43129943	28.66303319	28.89732825
37	28.55576101	28.79316551	29.03326124	29.27608224	29.52166298
38	29.12742459	29.37566461	29.62679558	29.88085513	30.13788136
39	29.69051322	29.94971747	30.21202045	30.47746358	30.74608891
40	30.24515553	30.51544657	30.78905216	31.06601783	31.34638975

i	-1.25	-1.20	-1.15	-1.10	-1.05
Years					
1	1.00000000	1.00000000	1.00000000	1.00000000	1.00000000
2	1.98750000	1.98800000	1.98850000	1.98900000	1.98950000
3	2.96265625	2.96414400	2.96563225	2.96712100	2.96861025
4	3.92562305	3.92857427	3.93152748	3.93448267	3.93743984
5	4.87655276	4.88143138	4.88631491	4.89120336	4.89609672
6	5.81559585	5.82285420	5.83012229	5.83740012	5.84468771
7	6.74290090	6.75297995	6.76307589	6.77318872	6.78331849
8	7.65861464	7.67194419	7.68530051	7.69868365	7.71209364
9	8.56288196	8.57988086	8.59691956	8.61399813	8.63111666
10	9.45584593	9.47692229	9.49805498	9.51924415	9.54048994
11	10.33764786	10.36319923	10.38882735	10.41453246	10.44031479
12	11.20842726	11.23884084	11.26935583	11.29997260	11.33069149
13	12.06832192	12.10397475	12.13975824	12.17567290	12.21171922
14	12.91746790	12.95872705	13.00015102	13.04174050	13.08349617
15	13.75599955	13.80322232	13.85064929	13.89828136	13.94611946
16	14.58404955	14.63758366	14.69136682	14.74540026	14.79968521
17	15.40174893	15.46193265	15.52241610	15.58320086	15.64428851
18	16.20922707	16.27638946	16.34390832	16.41178565	16.48002348
19	17.00661173	17.08107279	17.15595337	17.23125601	17.30698324
20	17.79402909	17.87609991	17.95865991	18.04171219	18.12525991
21	18.57160372	18.66158671	18.75213532	18.84325336	18.93494469
22	19.33945868	19.43764767	19.53648576	19.63597757	19.73612777
23	20.09771544	20.20439590	20.31181618	20.41998182	20.52889842
24	20.84649400	20.96194315	21.07823029	21.19536202	21.31334499
25	21.58591282	21.71039983	21.83583064	21.96221304	22.08955487
26	22.31608891	22.44987504	22.58471859	22.72062869	22.85761454
27	23.03713780	23.18047653	23.32499432	23.47070178	23.61760959
28	23.74917358	23.90231082	24.05675689	24.21252406	24.36962469
29	24.45230891	24.61548309	24.78010419	24.94618629	25.11374363
30	25.14665505	25.32009729	25.49513299	25.67177824	25.85004932
31	25.83232186	26.01625612	26.20193896	26.38938868	26.57862380
32	26.50941784	26.70406105	26.90061666	27.09910541	27.29954825
33	27.17805011	27.38361232	27.59125957	27.80101525	28.01290300
34	27.83832449	28.05500897	28.27396008	28.49520408	28.71876752
35	28.49034543	28.71834886	28.94880954	29.18175683	29.41722046
36	29.13421611	29.37372867	29.61589823	29.86075751	30.10833964
37	29.77003841	30.02124393	30.27531540	30.53228918	30.79220208
38	30.39791293	30.66098900	30.92714928	31.19643400	31.46888395
39	31.01793902	31.29305713	31.57148706	31.85327322	32.13846067
40	31.63021478	31.91754045	32.20841496	32.50288722	32.80100684

i	-1.00	-0.95	-0.90	-0.85	-0.80
Years					
1	1.00000000	1.00000000	1.00000000	1.00000000	1.00000000
2	1.99000000	1.99050000	1.99100000	1.99150000	1.99200000
3	2.97010000	2.97159025	2.97308100	2.97457225	2.97606400
4	3.94039900	3.94336014	3.94632327	3.94928839	3.95225549
5	4.90099501	4.90589822	4.91080636	4.91571943	4.92063744
6	5.85198506	5.85929219	5.86660910	5.87393582	5.88127234
7	6.79346521	6.80362891	6.81380962	6.82400736	6.83422217
8	7.72553056	7.73899444	7.75248534	7.76600330	7.77954839
9	8.64827525	8.66547399	8.68271297	8.69999227	8.71731200
10	9.56179250	9.58315199	9.60456855	9.62604234	9.64757351
11	10.46617457	10.49211204	10.51812743	10.54422098	10.57039292
12	11.36151283	11.39243698	11.42346429	11.45459510	11.48582977
13	12.24789770	12.28420883	12.32065311	12.35723104	12.39394314
14	13.12541872	13.16750884	13.20976723	13.25219458	13.29479159
15	13.99416454	14.04241751	14.09087933	14.13955093	14.18843326
16	14.85422289	14.90901454	14.96406141	15.01936474	15.07492579
17	15.70568066	15.76737891	15.82938486	15.89170014	15.95432639
18	16.54862385	16.61758881	16.68692040	16.75662069	16.82669177
19	17.38313762	17.45972171	17.53673811	17.61418942	17.69207824
20	18.20930624	18.29385436	18.37890747	18.46446881	18.55054161
21	19.02721318	19.12006274	19.21349730	19.30752082	19.40213728
22	19.83694105	19.93842214	20.04057583	20.14340689	20.24692018
23	20.63857164	20.74900713	20.86021064	20.97218793	21.08494482
24	21.43218592	21.55189157	21.67246875	21.79392434	21.91626526
25	22.21786406	22.34714860	22.47741653	22.60867598	22.74093514
26	22.99568542	23.13485068	23.27511978	23.41650223	23.55900766
27	23.76572857	23.91506960	24.06564370	24.21746197	24.37053560
28	24.52807128	24.68787644	24.84905291	25.01161354	25.17557131
29	25.28279057	25.45334162	25.62541143	25.79901482	25.97416674
30	26.02996266	26.21153487	26.39478273	26.57972320	26.76637341
31	26.76966303	26.96252529	27.15722968	27.35379555	27.55224242
32	27.50196640	27.70638130	27.91281462	28.12128829	28.33182448
33	28.22694674	28.44317068	28.66159929	28.88225734	29.10516989
34	28.94467727	29.17296055	29.40364489	29.63675815	29.87232853
35	29.65523050	29.89581743	30.13901209	30.38484571	30.63334990
36	30.35867820	30.61180716	30.86776098	31.12657452	31.38828310
37	31.05509141	31.32099500	31.58995113	31.86199863	32.13717684
38	31.74454050	32.02344554	32.30564157	32.59117165	32.88007942
39	32.42709509	32.71922281	33.01489080	33.31414669	33.61703879
40	33.10282414	33.40839019	33.71775678	34.03097644	34.34810248

i	-0.75	-0.70	-0.65	-0.60	-0.55
Years					
1	1.00000000	1.00000000	1.00000000	1.00000000	1.00000000
2	1.99250000	1.99300000	1.99350000	1.99400000	1.99450000
3	2.97755625	2.97904900	2.98054225	2.98203600	2.98353025
4	3.95522458	3.95819566	3.96116873	3.96414378	3.96712083
5	4.92556039	4.93048829	4.93542113	4.94035892	4.94530167
6	5.88861869	5.89597487	5.90334089	5.91071677	5.91810251
7	6.84445405	6.85470305	6.86496918	6.87525247	6.88555295
8	7.79312065	7.80672012	7.82034688	7.83400095	7.84768240
9	8.73467224	8.75207308	8.76951462	8.78699695	8.80452015
10	9.66916220	9.69080857	9.71251278	9.73427496	9.75609529
11	10.59664348	10.62297291	10.64938144	10.67586932	10.70243677
12	11.51716866	11.54861210	11.58016046	11.61181410	11.64357336
13	12.43078989	12.46777182	12.50488942	12.54214321	12.57953371
14	13.33755897	13.38049741	13.42360764	13.46689036	13.51034628
15	14.23752727	14.28683393	14.33635419	14.38608901	14.43603937
16	15.13074582	15.18682609	15.24316789	15.29977248	15.35664115
17	16.01726523	16.08051831	16.14408730	16.20797384	16.27217963
18	16.89713574	16.96795468	17.03915073	17.11072600	17.18268264
19	17.77040722	17.84917900	17.92839625	18.00806165	18.08817789
20	18.63712917	18.72423475	18.81186167	18.90001328	18.98869291
21	19.49735070	19.59316510	19.68958457	19.78661320	19.88425510
22	20.35112057	20.45601295	20.56160227	20.66789352	20.77489169
23	21.19848716	21.31282086	21.42795186	21.54388616	21.66062979
24	22.03949851	22.16363111	22.28867017	22.41462284	22.54149633
25	22.87420227	23.00848569	23.14379381	23.28013510	23.41751810
26	23.70264575	23.84742629	23.99335916	24.14045429	24.28872175
27	24.52487591	24.68049431	24.83740232	24.99561157	25.15513378
28	25.34093934	25.50773085	25.67595921	25.84563790	26.01678054
29	26.15088229	26.32917673	26.50906547	26.69056407	26.87368825
30	26.95475068	27.14487250	27.33675655	27.53042068	27.72588296
31	27.75259005	27.95485839	28.15906763	28.36523816	28.57339061
32	28.54444562	28.75917438	28.97603369	29.19504673	29.41623696
33	29.33036228	29.55786016	29.78768947	30.01987645	30.25444765
34	30.11038456	30.35095514	30.59406949	30.83975719	31.08804819
35	30.88455668	31.13849845	31.39520804	31.65471865	31.91706393
36	31.65292250	31.92052896	32.19113918	32.46479034	32.74152008
37	32.41552558	32.69708526	32.98189678	33.27000159	33.56144172
38	33.17240914	33.46820566	33.76751445	34.07038159	34.37685379
39	33.92361607	34.23392822	34.54802561	34.86595930	35.18778109
40	34.66918895	34.99429073	35.32346344	35.65676354	35.99424829

i	-0.50	-0.45	-0.40	-0.35	-0.30
Years					
1	1.00000000	1.00000000	1.00000000	1.00000000	1.00000000
2	1.99500000	1.99550000	1.99600000	1.99650000	1.99700000
3	2.98502500	2.98652025	2.98801600	2.98951225	2.99100900
4	3.97009987	3.97308091	3.97606394	3.97904896	3.98203597
5	4.95024938	4.95520204	4.96015968	4.96512229	4.97008987
6	5.92549813	5.93290364	5.94031904	5.94774436	5.95517960
7	6.89587064	6.90620557	6.91655777	6.92692725	6.93731406
8	7.86139128	7.87512764	7.88889153	7.90268301	7.91650211
9	8.82208433	8.83968957	8.85733597	8.87502362	8.89275261
10	9.77797391	9.79991097	9.82190662	9.84396103	9.86607435
11	10.72908404	10.75581137	10.78261900	10.80950717	10.83647613
12	11.67543862	11.70741022	11.73948852	11.77167390	11.80396670
13	12.61706142	12.65472687	12.69253057	12.73047304	12.76855480
14	13.55397612	13.59778060	13.64176045	13.68591638	13.73024913
15	14.48620624	14.53659059	14.58719340	14.63801567	14.68905839
16	15.41377521	15.47117593	15.52884463	15.58678262	15.64499121
17	16.33670633	16.40155564	16.46672925	16.53222888	16.59805624
18	17.25502280	17.32774864	17.40086233	17.47436608	17.54826207
19	18.16874768	18.24977377	18.33125889	18.41320580	18.49561728
20	19.07790395	19.16764979	19.25793385	19.34875958	19.44013043
21	19.98251443	20.08139536	20.18090211	20.28103892	20.38181004
22	20.88260185	20.99102908	21.10017851	21.21005528	21.32066461
23	21.77818884	21.89656945	22.01577779	22.13582009	22.25670262
24	22.66929790	22.79803489	22.92771468	23.05834472	23.18993251
25	23.55595141	23.69544373	23.83600382	23.97764051	24.12036271
26	24.43817165	24.58881424	24.74065981	24.89371877	25.04800162
27	25.31598079	25.47816457	25.64169717	25.80659075	25.97285762
28	26.18940089	26.36351283	26.53913038	26.71626769	26.89493904
29	27.05845389	27.24487702	27.43297386	27.62276075	27.81425423
30	27.92316162	28.12227508	28.32324196	28.52608109	28.73081147
31	28.78354581	28.99572484	29.20994899	29.42623980	29.64461903
32	29.63962808	29.86524408	30.09310920	30.32324796	30.55568517
33	30.49142994	30.73085048	30.97273676	31.21711660	31.46401812
34	31.33897279	31.59256165	31.84884581	32.10785669	32.36962606
35	32.18227793	32.45039512	32.72145043	32.99547919	33.27251719
36	33.02136654	33.30436835	33.59056463	33.87999501	34.17269963
37	33.85625970	34.15449869	34.45620237	34.76141503	35.07018154
38	34.68697841	35.00080344	35.31837756	35.63975008	35.96497099
39	35.51354351	35.84329983	36.17710405	36.51501095	36.85707608
40	36.33597580	36.68200498	37.03239563	37.38720841	37.74650485

i	-0.25	-0.20	-0.15	-0.10	-0.05
Years					
1	1.00000000	1.00000000	1.00000000	1.00000000	1.00000000
2	1.99750000	1.99800000	1.99850000	1.99900000	1.99950000
3	2.99250625	2.99400400	2.99550225	2.99700100	2.99850025
4	3.98502498	3.98801599	3.99100900	3.99400400	3.99700100
5	4.97506242	4.98003996	4.98502248	4.99001000	4.99500250
6	5.96262477	5.97007988	5.97754495	5.98501999	5.99250500
7	6.94771820	6.95813972	6.96857863	6.97903497	6.98950875
8	7.93034891	7.94422344	7.95812576	7.97205593	7.98601399
9	8.91052304	8.92833499	8.94618858	8.96408387	8.98202098
10	9.88824673	9.91047832	9.93276929	9.95511979	9.97752997
11	10.86352611	10.89065737	10.91787014	10.94516467	10.97254121
12	11.83636730	11.86887605	11.90149333	11.93421951	11.96705494
13	12.80677638	12.84513830	12.88364109	12.92228529	12.96107141
14	13.77475944	13.81944802	13.86431563	13.90936300	13.95459087
15	14.74032254	14.79180913	14.84351916	14.89545364	14.94761358
16	15.70347173	15.76222551	15.82125388	15.88055818	15.94013977
17	16.66421305	16.73070106	16.79752200	16.86467763	16.93216970
18	17.62255252	17.69723966	17.77232572	17.84781295	17.92370362
19	18.57849614	18.66184518	18.74566723	18.82996514	18.91474177
20	19.53204990	19.62452149	19.71754873	19.81113517	19.90528440
21	20.48321977	20.58527244	20.68797240	20.79132404	20.89533175
22	21.43201172	21.54410190	21.65694044	21.77053271	21.88488409
23	22.37843170	22.50101370	22.62445503	22.74876218	22.87394165
24	23.32248562	23.45601167	23.59051835	23.72601342	23.86250467
25	24.26417940	24.40909964	24.55513257	24.70228740	24.85057342
26	25.20351895	25.36028145	25.51829988	25.67758512	25.83814814
27	26.14051016	26.30956088	26.48002243	26.65190753	26.82522906
28	27.07515888	27.25694176	27.44030239	27.62525562	27.81181645
29	28.00747098	28.20242788	28.39914194	28.59763037	28.79791054
30	28.93745231	29.14602302	29.35654323	29.56903274	29.78351158
31	29.86510868	30.08773098	30.31250841	30.53946370	30.76861983
32	30.79044590	31.02755551	31.26703965	31.50892424	31.75323552
33	31.71346979	31.96550040	32.22013909	32.47741532	32.73735890
34	32.63418611	32.90156940	33.17180888	33.44493790	33.72099022
35	33.55260065	33.83576626	34.12205117	34.41149296	34.70412973
36	34.46871915	34.76809473	35.07086809	35.37708147	35.68677766
37	35.38254735	35.69855854	36.01826179	36.34170439	36.66893427
38	36.29409098	36.62716142	36.96423439	37.30536268	37.65059980
39	37.20335575	37.55390710	37.90878804	38.26805732	38.63177450
40	38.11034736	38.47879929	38.85192486	39.22978926	39.61245862

Uniform Series Compound Amount (USCA) Factors

for positive interest rates

i	0.00	0.05	0.10	0.15	0.20
Years					
1	1.00000000	1.00000000	1.00000000	1.00000000	1.00000000
2	2.00000000	2.00050000	2.00100000	2.00150000	2.00200000
3	3.00000000	3.00150025	3.00300100	3.00450225	3.00600400
4	4.00000000	4.00300100	4.00600400	4.00900900	4.01201601
5	5.00000000	5.00500250	5.01001001	5.01502252	5.02004004
6	6.00000000	6.00750500	6.01502002	6.02254505	6.03008012
7	7.00000000	7.01050875	7.02103504	7.03157887	7.04214028
8	8.00000000	8.01401401	8.02805607	8.04212624	8.05622456
9	9.00000000	9.01802102	9.03608413	9.05418943	9.07233701
10	10.00000000	10.02253003	10.04512021	10.06777071	10.09048168
11	11.00000000	11.02754129	11.05516533	11.08287237	11.11066265
12	12.00000000	12.03305506	12.06622050	12.09949667	12.13288397
13	13.00000000	13.03907159	13.07828672	13.11764592	13.15714974
14	14.00000000	14.04559113	14.09136500	14.13732239	14.18346404
15	15.00000000	15.05261392	15.10545637	15.15852837	15.21183097
16	16.00000000	16.06014023	16.12056182	16.18126616	16.24225463
17	17.00000000	17.06817030	17.13668239	17.20553806	17.27473914
18	18.00000000	18.07670438	18.15381907	18.23134637	18.30928862
19	19.00000000	19.08574274	19.17197289	19.25869339	19.34590719
20	20.00000000	20.09528561	20.19114486	20.28758143	20.38459901
21	21.00000000	21.10533325	21.21133601	21.31801280	21.42536821
22	22.00000000	22.11588592	22.23254734	22.34998982	22.46821894
23	23.00000000	23.12694386	23.25477989	23.38351481	23.51315538
24	24.00000000	24.13850733	24.27803467	24.41859008	24.56018169
25	25.00000000	25.15057658	25.30231270	25.45521796	25.60930206
26	26.00000000	26.16315187	26.32761502	26.49340079	26.66052066
27	27.00000000	27.17623345	27.35394263	27.53314089	27.71384170
28	28.00000000	28.18982157	28.38129657	28.57444060	28.76926938
29	29.00000000	29.20391648	29.40967787	29.61730226	29.82680792
30	30.00000000	30.21851843	30.43908755	30.66172822	30.88646154
31	31.00000000	31.23362769	31.46952664	31.70772081	31.94823446
32	32.00000000	32.24924451	32.50099616	32.75528239	33.01213093
33	33.00000000	33.26536913	33.53349716	33.80441531	34.07815519
34	34.00000000	34.28200181	34.56703066	34.85512194	35.14631150
35	35.00000000	35.29914282	35.60159769	35.90740462	36.21660413
36	36.00000000	36.31679239	36.63719928	36.96126573	37.28903733
37	37.00000000	37.33495078	37.67383648	38.01670763	38.36361541
38	38.00000000	38.35361826	38.71151032	39.07373269	39.44034264
39	39.00000000	39.37279507	39.75022183	40.13234329	40.51922333
40	40.00000000	40.39248146	40.78997205	41.19254180	41.60026177

i	0.25	0.30	0.35	0.40	0.45
Years					
1	1.00000000	1.00000000	1.00000000	1.00000000	1.00000000
2	2.00250000	2.00300000	2.00350000	2.00400000	2.00450000
3	3.00750625	3.00900900	3.01051225	3.01201600	3.01352025
4	4.01502502	4.01803603	4.02104904	4.02406406	4.02708109
5	5.02506258	5.03009014	5.03512271	5.04016032	5.04520296
6	6.03762523	6.04518041	6.05274564	6.06032096	6.06790637
7	7.05271930	7.06331595	7.07393025	7.08456225	7.09521195
8	8.07035110	8.08450589	8.09868901	8.11290049	8.12714040
9	9.09052697	9.10875941	9.12703442	9.14535210	9.16371253
10	10.11325329	10.13608569	10.15897904	10.18193350	10.20494924
11	11.13853642	11.16649395	11.19453547	11.22266124	11.25087151
12	12.16638277	12.19999343	12.23371634	12.26755188	12.30150043
13	13.19679872	13.23659341	13.27653435	13.31662209	13.35685719
14	14.22979072	14.27630319	14.32300222	14.36988858	14.41696304
15	15.26536520	15.31913210	15.37313273	15.42736813	15.48183938
16	16.30352861	16.36508950	16.42693869	16.48907761	16.55150765
17	17.34428743	17.41418476	17.48443298	17.55503392	17.62598944
18	18.38764815	18.46642732	18.54562849	18.62525405	18.70530639
19	19.43361727	19.52182660	19.61053819	19.69975507	19.78948027
20	20.48220131	20.58039208	20.67917508	20.77855409	20.87853293
21	21.53340682	21.64213326	21.75155219	21.86166831	21.97248633
22	22.58724033	22.70705966	22.82768262	22.94911498	23.07136252
23	23.64370843	23.77518084	23.90757951	24.04091144	24.17518365
24	24.70281770	24.84650638	24.99125604	25.13707508	25.28397197
25	25.76457475	25.92104590	26.07872544	26.23762338	26.39774985
26	26.82898619	26.99880903	27.17000097	27.34257388	27.51653972
27	27.89605865	28.07980546	28.26509598	28.45194417	28.64036415
28	28.96579880	29.16404488	29.36402381	29.56575195	29.76924579
29	30.03821330	30.25153701	30.46679790	30.68401496	30.90320740
30	31.11330883	31.34229162	31.57343169	31.80675102	32.04227183
31	32.19109210	32.43631850	32.68393870	32.93397802	33.18646205
32	33.27156983	33.53362745	33.79833249	34.06571393	34.33580113
33	34.35474876	34.63422834	34.91662665	35.20197679	35.49031224
34	35.44063563	35.73813102	36.03883484	36.34278470	36.65001864
35	36.52923722	36.84534541	37.16497077	37.48815584	37.81494373
36	37.62056031	37.95588145	38.29504816	38.63810846	38.98511097
37	38.71461171	39.06974910	39.42908083	39.79266089	40.16054397
38	39.81139824	40.18695834	40.56708261	40.95183154	41.34126642
39	40.91092673	41.30751922	41.70906740	42.11563886	42.52730212
40	42.01320405	42.43144178	42.85504914	43.28410142	43.71867498

i	0.50	0.55	0.60	0.65	0.70
Years					
1	1.00000000	1.00000000	1.00000000	1.00000000	1.00000000
2	2.00500000	2.00550000	2.00600000	2.00650000	2.00700000
3	3.01502500	3.01653025	3.01803600	3.01954225	3.02104900
4	4.03010012	4.03312117	4.03614422	4.03916927	4.04219634
5	5.05025063	5.05530333	5.06036108	5.06542387	5.07049172
6	6.07550188	6.08310750	6.09072325	6.09834913	6.10598516
7	7.10587939	7.11656459	7.12726759	7.13798840	7.14872706
8	8.14140879	8.15570570	8.17003119	8.18438532	8.19876814
9	9.18211583	9.20056208	9.21905138	9.23758383	9.25615952
10	10.22802641	10.25116517	10.27436569	10.29762812	10.32095264
11	11.27916654	11.30754658	11.33601188	11.36456271	11.39319931
12	12.33556237	12.36973809	12.40402795	12.43843236	12.47295170
13	13.39724018	13.43777164	13.47845212	13.51928217	13.56026236
14	14.46422639	14.51167939	14.55932283	14.60715751	14.65518420
15	15.53654752	15.59149363	15.64667877	15.70210403	15.75777049
16	16.61423026	16.67724684	16.74055884	16.80416771	16.86807488
17	17.69730141	17.76897170	17.84100220	17.91339480	17.98615141
18	18.78578791	18.86670104	18.94804821	19.02983186	19.11205447
19	19.87971685	19.97046790	20.06173650	20.15352577	20.24583885
20	20.97911544	21.08030547	21.18210692	21.28452369	21.38755972
21	22.08401101	22.19624715	22.30919956	22.42287309	22.53727264
22	23.19443107	23.31832651	23.44305476	23.56862177	23.69503355
23	24.31040322	24.44657731	24.58371309	24.72181781	24.86089878
24	25.43195524	25.58103348	25.73121536	25.88250963	26.03492507
25	26.55911502	26.72172917	26.88560266	27.05074594	27.21716955
26	27.69191059	27.86869868	28.04691627	28.22657579	28.40768974
27	28.83037015	29.02197652	29.21519777	29.41004853	29.60654356
28	29.97452200	30.18159739	30.39048896	30.60121384	30.81378937
29	31.12439461	31.34759618	31.57283189	31.80012173	32.02948589
30	32.28001658	32.52000795	32.76226888	33.00682253	33.25369230
31	33.44141666	33.69886800	33.95884249	34.22136687	34.48646814
32	34.60862375	34.88421177	35.16259555	35.44380576	35.72787342
33	35.78166686	36.07607494	36.37357112	36.67419049	36.97796853
34	36.96057520	37.27449335	37.59181255	37.91257273	38.23681431
35	38.14537807	38.47950306	38.81736343	39.15900446	39.50447201
36	39.33610496	39.69114033	40.05026761	40.41353798	40.78100332
37	40.53278549	40.90944160	41.29056921	41.67622598	42.06647034
38	41.73544942	42.13444353	42.53831263	42.94712145	43.36093563
39	42.94412666	43.36618297	43.79354250	44.22627774	44.66446218
40	44.15884730	44.60469698	45.05630376	45.51374855	45.97711342

i	0.75	0.80	0.85	0.90	0.95
Years					
1	1.00000000	1.00000000	1.00000000	1.00000000	1.00000000
2	2.00750000	2.00800000	2.00850000	2.00900000	2.00950000
3	3.02255625	3.02406400	3.02557225	3.02708100	3.02859025
4	4.04522542	4.04825651	4.05128961	4.05432473	4.05736186
5	5.07556461	5.08064256	5.08572558	5.09081365	5.09590680
6	6.11363135	6.12128770	6.12895424	6.13663097	6.14431791
7	7.15948358	7.17025801	7.18105035	7.19186065	7.20268893
8	8.21317971	8.22762007	8.24208928	8.25658740	8.27111447
9	9.27477856	9.29344103	9.31214704	9.33089669	9.34969006
10	10.34433940	10.36778856	10.39130029	10.41487476	10.43851212
11	11.42192194	11.45073087	11.47962634	11.50860863	11.53767798
12	12.50758636	12.54233671	12.57720317	12.61218611	12.64728592
13	13.60139325	13.64267541	13.68410939	13.72569578	13.76743514
14	14.70340370	14.75181681	14.80042432	14.84922704	14.89822577
15	15.81367923	15.86983135	15.92622793	15.98287009	16.03975892
16	16.93228183	16.99679000	17.06160087	17.12671592	17.19213663
17	18.05927394	18.13276432	18.20662448	18.28085636	18.35546193
18	19.19471849	19.27782643	19.36138078	19.44538407	19.52983881
19	20.33867888	20.43204904	20.52595252	20.62039252	20.71537228
20	21.49121897	21.59550544	21.70042312	21.80597606	21.91216832
21	22.65240312	22.76826948	22.88487671	23.00222984	23.12033392
22	23.82229614	23.95041563	24.07939817	24.20924991	24.33997709
23	25.00096336	25.14201896	25.28407305	25.42713316	25.57120687
24	26.18847059	26.34315511	26.49898767	26.65597736	26.81413334
25	27.38488412	27.55390035	27.72422907	27.89588115	28.06886761
26	28.59027075	28.77433155	28.95988501	29.14694408	29.33552185
27	29.80469778	30.00452621	30.20604404	30.40926658	30.61420931
28	31.02823301	31.24456242	31.46279541	31.68294998	31.90504429
29	32.26094476	32.49451892	32.73022917	32.96809653	33.20814221
30	33.50290184	33.75447507	34.00843612	34.26480940	34.52361957
31	34.75417361	35.02451087	35.29750783	35.57319268	35.85159395
32	36.01482991	36.30470696	36.59753664	36.89335142	37.19218409
33	37.28494113	37.59514461	37.90861570	38.22539158	38.54550984
34	38.56457819	38.89590577	39.23083894	39.56942010	39.91169219
35	39.85381253	40.20707301	40.56430107	40.92554489	41.29085326
36	41.15271612	41.52872960	41.90909763	42.29387479	42.68311637
37	42.46136149	42.86095943	43.26532496	43.67451966	44.08860597
38	43.77982170	44.20384711	44.63308022	45.06759034	45.50744773
39	45.10817037	45.55747789	46.01246140	46.47319865	46.93976848
40	46.44648164	46.92193771	47.40356732	47.89145744	48.38569628

i	1.00	1.05	1.10	1.15	1.20
Years					
1	1.00000000	1.00000000	1.00000000	1.00000000	1.00000000
2	2.01000000	2.01050000	2.01100000	2.01150000	2.01200000
3	3.03010000	3.03161025	3.03312100	3.03463225	3.03614400
4	4.06040100	4.06344216	4.06648533	4.06953052	4.07257773
5	5.10100501	5.10610830	5.11121667	5.11633012	5.12144866
6	6.15201506	6.15972244	6.16744005	6.17516792	6.18290604
7	7.21353521	7.22439952	7.23528189	7.24618235	7.25710092
8	8.28567056	8.30025572	8.31486999	8.32951345	8.34418613
9	9.36852727	9.38740840	9.40633356	9.42530285	9.44431636
10	10.46221254	10.48597619	10.50980323	10.53369383	10.55764816
11	11.56683467	11.59607894	11.62541107	11.65483131	11.68433994
12	12.68250301	12.71783777	12.75329059	12.78886187	12.82455202
13	13.80932804	13.85137507	13.89357679	13.93593378	13.97844664
14	14.94742132	14.99681450	15.04640613	15.09619702	15.14618800
15	16.09689554	16.15428106	16.21191660	16.26980329	16.32794226
16	17.25786449	17.32390101	17.39024768	17.45690603	17.52387756
17	18.43044314	18.50580197	18.58154041	18.65766045	18.73416409
18	19.61474757	19.70011289	19.78593735	19.87222354	19.95897406
19	20.81089504	20.90696407	21.00358266	21.10075411	21.19848175
20	22.01900399	22.12648720	22.23462207	22.34341278	22.45286353
21	23.23919403	23.35881531	23.47920291	23.60036203	23.72229789
22	24.47158598	24.60408287	24.73747415	24.87176619	25.00696547
23	25.71630183	25.86242574	26.00958636	26.15779151	26.30704905
24	26.97346485	27.13398121	27.29569181	27.45860611	27.62273364
25	28.24319950	28.41888802	28.59594442	28.77438008	28.95420645
26	29.52563150	29.71728634	29.91049981	30.10528545	30.30165692
27	30.82088781	31.02931785	31.23951531	31.45149623	31.66527681
28	32.12909669	32.35512569	32.58314998	32.81318844	33.04526013
29	33.45038766	33.69485451	33.94156463	34.19054011	34.44180325
30	34.78489153	35.04865048	35.31492184	35.58373132	35.85510489
31	36.13274045	36.41666131	36.70338598	36.99294423	37.28536615
32	37.49406785	37.79903625	38.10712322	38.41836309	38.73279054
33	38.86900853	39.19592613	39.52630158	39.86017426	40.19758403
34	40.25769862	40.60748336	40.96109090	41.31856626	41.67995504
35	41.66027560	42.03386193	42.41166290	42.79372978	43.18011450
36	43.07687836	43.47521748	43.87819119	44.28585767	44.69827587
37	44.50764714	44.93170727	45.36085129	45.79514503	46.23465518
38	45.95272361	46.40349019	46.85982065	47.32178920	47.78947104
39	47.41225085	47.89072684	48.37527868	48.86598978	49.36294470
40	48.88637336	49.39357947	49.90740675	50.42794866	50.95530003

i	1.25	1.30	1.35	1.40	1.45
Years					
1	1.00000000	1.00000000	1.00000000	1.00000000	1.00000000
2	2.01250000	2.01300000	2.01350000	2.01400000	2.01450000
3	3.03765625	3.03916900	3.04068225	3.04219600	3.04371025
4	4.07562695	4.07867820	4.08173146	4.08478674	4.08784405
5	5.12657229	5.13170101	5.13683484	5.14197376	5.14711779
6	6.19065444	6.19841313	6.20618211	6.21396139	6.22175100
7	7.26803762	7.27899250	7.28996556	7.30095685	7.31196638
8	8.35888809	8.37361940	8.38838010	8.40317025	8.41798990
9	9.46337420	9.48247645	9.50162323	9.52081463	9.54005075
10	10.58166637	10.60574865	10.62989514	10.65410603	10.67838149
11	11.71393720	11.74362338	11.77339873	11.80326352	11.83321802
12	12.86036142	12.89629048	12.93233961	12.96850921	13.00479968
13	14.02111594	14.06394226	14.10692620	14.15006834	14.19336927
14	15.19637988	15.24677351	15.29736970	15.34816929	15.39917313
15	16.38633463	16.44498156	16.50388419	16.56304366	16.62246114
16	17.59116382	17.65876632	17.72668663	17.79492628	17.86348683
17	18.81105336	18.88833029	18.96599690	19.04405524	19.12250739
18	20.04619153	20.13387858	20.22203785	20.31067202	20.39978374
19	21.29676893	21.39561900	21.49503537	21.59502142	21.69558061
20	22.56297854	22.67376205	22.78521834	22.89735172	23.01016653
21	23.84501577	23.96852095	24.09281879	24.21791465	24.34381394
22	25.14307847	25.28011173	25.41807184	25.55696545	25.69679924
23	26.45736695	26.60875318	26.76121581	26.91476297	27.06940283
24	27.78808403	27.95466697	28.12249223	28.29156965	28.46190917
25	29.13543508	29.31807764	29.50214587	29.68765163	29.87460686
26	30.49962802	30.69921265	30.90042484	31.10327875	31.30778865
27	31.88087337	32.09830242	32.31758058	32.53872465	32.76175159
28	33.27938429	33.51558035	33.75386792	33.99426680	34.23679699
29	34.69537659	34.95128289	35.20954513	35.47018653	35.73323054
30	36.12906880	36.40564957	36.68487399	36.96676914	37.25136239
31	37.58068216	37.87892301	38.18011979	38.48430391	38.79150714
32	39.05044069	39.37134901	39.69555141	40.02308417	40.35398400
33	40.53857120	40.88317655	41.23144135	41.58340735	41.93911676
34	42.04530334	42.41465784	42.78806581	43.16557505	43.54723396
35	43.57086963	43.96604840	44.36570470	44.76989310	45.17866885
36	45.11550550	45.53760703	45.96464171	46.39667160	46.83375955
37	46.67944932	47.12959592	47.58516437	48.04622500	48.51284906
38	48.26294243	48.74228066	49.22756409	49.71887215	50.21628537
39	49.86622921	50.37593031	50.89213621	51.41493636	51.94442151
40	51.48955708	52.03081741	52.57918005	53.13474547	53.69761562

i	1.50	1.55	1.60	1.65	1.70
Years					
1	1.00000000	1.00000000	1.00000000	1.00000000	1.00000000
2	2.01500000	2.01550000	2.01600000	2.01650000	2.01700000
3	3.04522500	3.04674025	3.04825600	3.04977225	3.05128900
4	4.09090337	4.09396472	4.09702810	4.10009349	4.10316091
5	5.15226693	5.15742118	5.16258055	5.16774503	5.17291465
6	6.22955093	6.23736121	6.24518183	6.25301283	6.26085420
7	7.32299419	7.33404030	7.34510474	7.35618754	7.36728872
8	8.43283911	8.44771793	8.46262642	8.47756463	8.49253263
9	9.55933169	9.57865756	9.59802844	9.61744445	9.63690568
10	10.70272167	10.72712675	10.75159690	10.77613228	10.80073308
11	11.86326249	11.89339721	11.92362245	11.95393847	11.98434554
12	13.04121143	13.07774487	13.11440041	13.15117845	13.18807941
13	14.23682960	14.28044992	14.32423081	14.36817290	14.41227676
14	15.45038205	15.50179689	15.55341851	15.60524775	15.65728547
15	16.68213778	16.74207474	16.80227320	16.86273434	16.92345932
16	17.93236984	18.00157690	18.07110957	18.14096945	18.21115813
17	19.20135539	19.28060134	19.36024733	19.44029545	19.52074782
18	20.48937572	20.57945066	20.67001128	20.76106032	20.85260053
19	21.79671636	21.89843215	22.00073146	22.10361782	22.20709474
20	23.12366710	23.23785785	23.35274317	23.46832751	23.58461535
21	24.47052211	24.59804464	24.72638706	24.85555492	24.98555381
22	25.83757994	25.97931433	26.12200925	26.26567157	26.41030823
23	27.22514364	27.38199371	27.53996140	27.69905515	27.85928347
24	28.63352080	28.80641461	28.98060078	29.15608956	29.33289129
25	30.06302361	30.25291404	30.44429039	30.63716504	30.83155044
26	31.51396896	31.72183420	31.93139904	32.14267827	32.35568680
27	32.98667850	33.21352263	33.44230143	33.67303246	33.90573347
28	34.48147867	34.72833223	34.97737825	35.22863749	35.48213094
29	35.99870085	36.26662138	36.53701630	36.80991001	37.08532717
30	37.53868137	37.82875402	38.12160856	38.41727353	38.71577773
31	39.10176159	39.41509970	39.73155430	40.05115854	40.37394595
32	40.68828801	41.02603375	41.36725917	41.71200265	42.06030303
33	42.29861233	42.66193727	43.02913531	43.40025070	43.77532818
34	43.93309152	44.32319730	44.71760148	45.11635484	45.51950876
35	45.59208789	46.01020686	46.43308310	46.86077469	47.29334041
36	47.27596921	47.72336506	48.17601243	48.63397747	49.09732720
37	48.98510874	49.46307722	49.94682863	50.43643810	50.93198176
38	50.71988538	51.22975492	51.74597789	52.26863933	52.79782545
39	52.48068366	53.02381612	53.57391354	54.13107188	54.69538848
40	54.26789391	54.84568527	55.43109615	56.02423456	56.62521009

i	1.75	1.80	1.85	1.90	1.95
Years					
1	1.00000000	1.00000000	1.00000000	1.00000000	1.00000000
2	2.01750000	2.01800000	2.01850000	2.01900000	2.01950000
3	3.05280625	3.05432400	3.05584225	3.05736100	3.05888025
4	4.10623036	4.10930183	4.11237533	4.11545086	4.11852841
5	5.17808939	5.18326926	5.18845428	5.19364443	5.19883972
6	6.26870596	6.27656811	6.28444068	6.29232367	6.30021709
7	7.37840831	7.38954634	7.40070283	7.41187782	7.42307133
8	8.50753045	8.52255817	8.53761583	8.55270350	8.56782122
9	9.65641224	9.67596422	9.69556173	9.71520486	9.73489373
10	10.82539945	10.85013157	10.87492962	10.89979376	10.92472416
11	12.01484394	12.04543394	12.07611582	12.10688984	12.13775628
12	13.22510371	13.26225175	13.29952396	13.33692074	13.37444253
13	14.45654303	14.50097229	14.54556515	14.59032224	14.63524416
14	15.70953253	15.76198979	15.81465811	15.86753836	15.92063142
15	16.98444935	17.04570560	17.10722928	17.16902159	17.23108373
16	18.28167721	18.35252830	18.42371303	18.49523300	18.56708986
17	19.60160656	19.68287381	19.76455172	19.84664243	19.92914812
18	20.94463468	21.03716554	21.13019592	21.22372863	21.31776650
19	22.31116578	22.41583452	22.52110455	22.62697948	22.73346295
20	23.70161119	23.81931954	23.93774498	24.05689209	24.17676548
21	25.11638938	25.24806729	25.38059326	25.51397304	25.64821241
22	26.55592620	26.70253251	26.85013424	26.99873853	27.14835255
23	28.02065490	28.18317809	28.34686172	28.51171456	28.67774542
24	29.51101637	29.69047530	29.87127866	30.05343713	30.23696146
25	31.02745915	31.22490385	31.42389732	31.62445244	31.82658221
26	32.57043969	32.78695212	33.00523942	33.22531704	33.44720056
27	34.14042238	34.37711726	34.61583635	34.85659806	35.09942097
28	35.73787977	35.99590537	36.25622932	36.51887342	36.78385968
29	37.36329267	37.64383167	37.92696956	38.21273202	38.50114494
30	39.01715029	39.32142064	39.62861850	39.93877393	40.25191727
31	40.69995042	41.02920621	41.36174794	41.69761063	42.03682966
32	42.41219955	42.76773192	43.12694028	43.48986523	43.85654783
33	44.15441305	44.53755110	44.92478868	45.31617267	45.71175052
34	45.92711527	46.33922701	46.75589727	47.17717995	47.60312965
35	47.73083979	48.17333310	48.62088137	49.07354637	49.53139068
36	49.56612949	50.04045310	50.52036767	51.00594375	51.49725280
37	51.43353675	51.94118125	52.45499447	52.97505668	53.50144923
38	53.33362365	53.87612252	54.42541187	54.98158276	55.54472749
39	55.26696206	55.84589272	56.43228199	57.02623283	57.62784967
40	57.23413390	57.85111879	58.47627921	59.10973126	59.75159274

i	2.00	2.05	2.10	2.15	2.20
Years					
1	1.00000000	1.00000000	1.00000000	1.00000000	1.00000000
2	2.02000000	2.02050000	2.02100000	2.02150000	2.02200000
3	3.06040000	3.06192025	3.06344100	3.06496225	3.06648400
4	4.12160800	4.12468962	4.12777326	4.13085894	4.13394665
5	5.20404016	5.20924575	5.21445650	5.21967241	5.22489347
6	6.30812096	6.31603529	6.32396009	6.33189536	6.33984113
7	7.43428338	7.44551401	7.45676325	7.46803111	7.47931764
8	8.58296905	8.59814705	8.61335528	8.62859378	8.64386262
9	9.75462843	9.77440907	9.79423574	9.81410855	9.83402760
10	10.94972100	10.97478445	10.99991469	11.02511188	11.05037621
11	12.16871542	12.19976753	12.23091290	12.26215179	12.29348449
12	13.41208973	13.44986277	13.48776207	13.52578805	13.56394114
13	14.68033152	14.72558495	14.77100507	14.81659249	14.86234785
14	15.97393815	16.02745945	16.08119618	16.13514923	16.18931950
15	17.29341692	17.35602236	17.41890130	17.48205494	17.54548453
16	18.63928525	18.71182082	18.78469822	18.85791912	18.93148519
17	20.01207096	20.09541315	20.17917689	20.26336438	20.34797786
18	21.41231238	21.50736912	21.60293960	21.69902672	21.79563338
19	22.84055863	22.94827019	23.05660133	23.16555579	23.27513731
20	24.29736980	24.41870972	24.54078996	24.66361524	24.78719033
21	25.78331719	25.91929327	26.05614655	26.19388297	26.33250852
22	27.29898354	27.45063879	27.60332563	27.75705145	27.91182371
23	28.84496321	29.01337688	29.18299547	29.35382806	29.52588383
24	30.42186247	30.60815111	30.79583837	30.98493536	31.17545327
25	32.03029972	32.23561820	32.44255098	32.65111147	32.86131325
26	33.67090572	33.89644838	34.12384455	34.35311037	34.58426214
27	35.34432383	35.59132557	35.84044528	36.09170224	36.34511590
28	37.05121031	37.32094774	37.59309463	37.86767384	38.14470845
29	38.79223451	39.08602717	39.38254962	39.68182883	39.98389204
30	40.56807921	40.88729073	41.20958316	41.53498815	41.86353766
31	42.37944079	42.72548019	43.07498441	43.42799039	43.78453549
32	44.22702961	44.60135253	44.97955908	45.36169219	45.74779527
33	46.11157020	46.51568026	46.92412982	47.33696857	47.75424677
34	48.03380160	48.46925171	48.90953655	49.35471339	49.80484020
35	49.99447763	50.46287137	50.93663682	51.41583973	51.90054668
36	51.99436719	52.49736023	53.00630619	53.52128028	54.04235871
37	54.03425453	54.57355611	55.11943862	55.67198781	56.23129060
38	56.11493962	56.69231401	57.27694683	57.86893555	58.46837900
39	58.23723841	58.85450645	59.47976271	60.11311766	60.75468333
40	60.40198318	61.06102383	61.72883773	62.40554969	63.09128637

i	2.25	2.30	2.35	2.40	2.45
Years					
1	1.00000000	1.00000000	1.00000000	1.00000000	1.00000000
2	2.02250000	2.02300000	2.02350000	2.02400000	2.02450000
3	3.06800625	3.06952900	3.07105225	3.07257600	3.07410025
4	4.13703639	4.14012817	4.14322198	4.14631782	4.14941571
5	5.23011971	5.23535111	5.24058769	5.24582945	5.25107639
6	6.34779740	6.35576419	6.36374151	6.37172936	6.37972776
7	7.49062284	7.50194677	7.51328943	7.52465086	7.53603109
8	8.65916186	8.67449154	8.68985173	8.70524248	8.72066385
9	9.85399300	9.87400485	9.89406325	9.91416830	9.93432012
10	11.07570784	11.10110696	11.12657373	11.15210834	11.17771096
11	12.32491127	12.35643242	12.38804822	12.41975894	12.45156488
12	13.60222177	13.64063037	13.67916735	13.71783316	13.75662822
13	14.90827176	14.95436486	15.00062778	15.04706115	15.09366561
14	16.24370788	16.29831526	16.35314254	16.40819062	16.46346042
15	17.60919130	17.67317651	17.73744139	17.80198720	17.86681520
16	19.00539811	19.07965957	19.15427126	19.22923489	19.30455217
17	20.43301957	20.51849174	20.60439663	20.69073653	20.77751370
18	21.89276251	21.99041705	22.08859995	22.18731420	22.28656279
19	23.38534966	23.49619664	23.60768205	23.71980974	23.83258357
20	24.91152003	25.03660916	25.16246258	25.28908518	25.41648187
21	26.47202923	26.61245117	26.75378045	26.89602322	27.03918568
22	28.06764989	28.22453755	28.38249429	28.54152778	28.70164573
23	29.69917201	29.87370191	30.04948291	30.22652445	30.40483605
24	31.36740338	31.56079706	31.75564576	31.95196103	32.14975453
25	33.07316996	33.28669539	33.50190343	33.71880810	33.93742352
26	34.81731628	35.05228938	35.28919816	35.52805949	35.76889039
27	36.60070590	36.85849204	37.11849432	37.38073292	37.64522821
28	38.42422178	38.70623735	38.99077893	39.27787051	39.56753630
29	40.28876677	40.59648081	40.90706224	41.22053940	41.53694094
30	42.19526402	42.53019987	42.86837820	43.20983235	43.55459599
31	44.14465746	44.50839447	44.87578509	45.24686832	45.62168359
32	46.13791226	46.53208754	46.93036604	47.33279316	47.73941484
33	48.17601528	48.60232556	49.03322964	49.46878020	49.90903050
34	50.25997563	50.72017904	51.18551054	51.65603092	52.13180175
35	52.39082508	52.88674316	53.38837004	53.89577567	54.40903089
36	54.56961864	55.10313825	55.64299673	56.18927428	56.74205215
37	56.79743506	57.37051043	57.95060716	58.53781687	59.13223243
38	59.07537735	59.69003217	60.31244642	60.94272447	61.58097212
39	61.40457334	62.06290291	62.72978891	63.40534986	64.08970594
40	63.78617624	64.49034968	65.20393895	65.92707825	66.65990373

i	2.50	2.55	2.60	2.65	2.70
Years					
1	1.00000000	1.00000000	1.00000000	1.00000000	1.00000000
2	2.02500000	2.02550000	2.02600000	2.02650000	2.02700000
3	3.07562500	3.07715025	3.07867600	3.08020225	3.08172900
4	4.15251563	4.15561758	4.15872158	4.16182761	4.16493568
5	5.25632852	5.26158583	5.26684834	5.27211604	5.27738895
6	6.38773673	6.39575627	6.40378639	6.41182712	6.41987845
7	7.54743015	7.55884805	7.57028484	7.58174053	7.59321517
8	8.73611590	8.75159868	8.76711225	8.78265666	8.79823198
9	9.95451880	9.97476444	9.99505716	10.01539706	10.03578424
10	11.20338177	11.22912094	11.25492865	11.28080508	11.30675041
11	12.48346631	12.51546352	12.54755680	12.57974642	12.61203267
12	13.79555297	13.83460784	13.87379327	13.91310970	13.95255756
13	15.14044179	15.18739034	15.23451190	15.28180710	15.32927661
14	16.51895284	16.57466880	16.63060921	16.68677499	16.74316708
15	17.93192666	17.99732285	18.06300505	18.12897453	18.19523259
16	19.38022483	19.45625458	19.53264318	19.60939236	19.68650387
17	20.86473045	20.95238907	21.04049190	21.12904125	21.21803947
18	22.38634871	22.48667500	22.58754469	22.68896085	22.79092654
19	23.94600743	24.06008521	24.17482085	24.29021831	24.40628156
20	25.54465761	25.67361738	25.80336619	25.93390909	26.06525116
21	27.18327405	27.32829462	27.47425371	27.62115768	27.76901294
22	28.86285590	29.02516614	29.18858431	29.35311836	29.51877629
23	30.58442730	30.76530787	30.94748750	31.13097600	31.31578325
24	32.34903798	32.54982322	32.75212218	32.95594686	33.16130940
25	34.15776393	34.37984372	34.60367735	34.82927946	35.05666475
26	36.01170803	36.25652973	36.50337297	36.75225536	37.00319470
27	37.91200073	38.18107124	38.45246066	38.72619013	39.00228096
28	39.85980075	40.15468856	40.45222464	40.75243417	41.05534254
29	41.85629577	42.17863311	42.50398248	42.83237367	43.16383679
30	43.90270316	44.25418826	44.60908603	44.96743157	45.32926038
31	46.00027074	46.38267006	46.76892226	47.15906851	47.55315041
32	48.15027751	48.56542815	48.98491424	49.40878383	49.83708548
33	50.35403445	50.80384656	51.25852201	51.71811660	52.18268678
34	52.61288531	53.09934465	53.59124358	54.08864669	54.59161933
35	54.92820744	55.45337794	55.98461592	56.52199582	57.06559305
36	57.30141263	57.86743908	58.44021593	59.01982871	59.60636406
37	59.73394794	60.34305877	60.95966154	61.58385418	62.21573589
38	62.22729664	62.88180677	63.54461274	64.21582631	64.89556076
39	64.78297906	65.48529284	66.19677268	66.91754571	67.64774090
40	67.40255354	68.15516781	68.91788877	69.69086067	70.47422990

i	2.75	2.80	2.85	2.90	2.95
Years					
1	1.00000000	1.00000000	1.00000000	1.00000000	1.00000000
2	2.02750000	2.02800000	2.02850000	2.02900000	2.02950000
3	3.08325625	3.08478400	3.08631225	3.08784100	3.08937025
4	4.16804580	4.17115795	4.17427215	4.17738839	4.18050667
5	5.28266706	5.28795037	5.29323891	5.29853265	5.30383162
6	6.42794040	6.43601299	6.44409621	6.45219010	6.46029465
7	7.60470876	7.61622135	7.62775296	7.63930361	7.65087334
8	8.81383825	8.82947555	8.84514392	8.86084342	8.87657411
9	10.05621880	10.07670086	10.09723052	10.11780788	10.13843304
10	11.33276482	11.35884849	11.38500159	11.41122430	11.43751682
11	12.64441585	12.67689624	12.70947413	12.74214981	12.77492357
12	13.99213729	14.03184934	14.07169414	14.11167215	14.15178381
13	15.37692107	15.42474112	15.47273743	15.52091065	15.56926143
14	16.79978639	16.85663387	16.91371044	16.97101705	17.02855464
15	18.26178052	18.32861962	18.39575119	18.46317655	18.53089701
16	19.76397948	19.84182097	19.92003010	19.99860867	20.07755847
17	21.30748892	21.39739196	21.48775096	21.57856832	21.66984644
18	22.89344487	22.99651893	23.10015186	23.20434680	23.30910691
19	24.52301460	24.64042146	24.75850619	24.87727286	24.99672557
20	26.19739750	26.33035326	26.46412362	26.59871377	26.73412897
21	27.91782593	28.06760315	28.21835114	28.37007647	28.52278578
22	29.68556615	29.85349604	30.02257415	30.19280869	30.36420796
23	31.50191921	31.68939393	31.87821751	32.06840014	32.25995209
24	33.36822199	33.57669696	33.78674671	33.99838375	34.21162068
25	35.28584810	35.51684448	35.74966899	35.98433687	36.22086349
26	37.25620892	37.51131612	37.76853456	38.02788264	38.28937896
27	39.28075467	39.56163297	39.84493779	40.13069124	40.41891564
28	41.36097542	41.66935870	41.98051852	42.29448129	42.61127365
29	43.49840224	43.83610074	44.17696330	44.52102124	44.86830622
30	45.69460831	46.06351156	46.43600675	46.81213086	47.19192126
31	47.95121003	48.35328988	48.75943294	49.16968265	49.58408294
32	50.26986831	50.70718200	51.14907678	51.59560345	52.04681338
33	52.65228969	53.12698310	53.60682547	54.09187595	54.58219438
34	55.10022765	55.61453862	56.13462000	56.66054035	57.19236911
35	57.61548391	58.17174570	58.73445666	59.30369602	59.87954400
36	60.19990972	60.80055458	61.40838868	62.02350321	62.64599055
37	62.85540724	63.50297011	64.15852776	64.82218480	65.49404727
38	65.58393094	66.28105328	66.98704580	67.70202816	68.42612166
39	68.38748904	69.13692277	69.89617660	70.66538698	71.44469225
40	71.26814499	72.07275660	72.88821764	73.71468320	74.55231067

i	3.00	3.05	3.10	3.15	3.20
Years					
1	1.00000000	1.00000000	1.00000000	1.00000000	1.00000000
2	2.03000000	2.03050000	2.03100000	2.03150000	2.03200000
3	3.09090000	3.09243025	3.09396100	3.09549225	3.09702400
4	4.18362700	4.18674937	4.18987379	4.19300026	4.19612877
5	5.30913581	5.31444523	5.31975988	5.32507976	5.33040489
6	6.46840988	6.47653581	6.48467243	6.49281978	6.50097785
7	7.66246218	7.67407015	7.68569728	7.69734360	7.70900914
8	8.89233605	8.90812929	8.92395390	8.93980992	8.95569743
9	10.15910613	10.17982723	10.20059647	10.22141394	10.24227975
10	11.46387931	11.49031196	11.51681496	11.54338847	11.57003270
11	12.80779569	12.84076648	12.87383622	12.90700521	12.94027374
12	14.19202956	14.23240986	14.27292514	14.31357588	14.35436250
13	15.61779045	15.66649836	15.71538582	15.76445352	15.81370210
14	17.08632416	17.14432656	17.20256278	17.26103380	17.31974057
15	18.59891389	18.66722852	18.73584223	18.80475637	18.87397227
16	20.15688130	20.23657899	20.31665334	20.39710619	20.47793938
17	21.76158774	21.85379465	21.94646959	22.03961504	22.13323344
18	23.41443537	23.52033538	23.62681015	23.73386291	23.84149691
19	25.11686844	25.23770561	25.35924126	25.48147959	25.60442481
20	26.87037449	27.00745563	27.14537774	27.28414620	27.42376641
21	28.67648572	28.83118303	28.98688445	29.14359680	29.30132693
22	30.53678030	30.71053411	30.88547787	31.06162010	31.23896940
23	32.45288370	32.64720540	32.84292769	33.04006114	33.23861642
24	34.42647022	34.64294517	34.86105844	35.08082306	35.30225214
25	36.45926432	36.69955499	36.94175126	37.18586899	37.43192421
26	38.55304225	38.81889142	39.08694554	39.35722386	39.62974578
27	40.70963352	41.00286761	41.29864086	41.59697641	41.89789765
28	42.93092252	43.25345507	43.57889872	43.90728117	44.23863037
29	45.21885020	45.57268545	45.92984458	46.29036053	46.65426655
30	47.57541571	47.96265236	48.35366977	48.74850688	49.14720308
31	50.00267818	50.42551326	50.85263353	51.28408485	51.71991357
32	52.50275852	52.96349141	53.42906517	53.89953352	54.37495081
33	55.07784128	55.57887790	56.08536619	56.59736883	57.11494923
34	57.73017652	58.27403367	58.82401254	59.38018595	59.94262761
35	60.46208181	61.05139170	61.64755693	62.25066181	62.86079169
36	63.27594427	63.91345915	64.55863119	65.21155765	65.87233703
37	66.17422259	66.86281965	67.55994876	68.26572172	68.98025181
38	69.15944927	69.90213565	70.65430717	71.41609195	72.18761987
39	72.23423275	73.03415079	73.84459069	74.66569885	75.49762371
40	75.40125973	76.26169239	77.13377301	78.01766836	78.91354766

i	3.25	3.30	3.35	3.40	3.45
Years					
1	1.00000000	1.00000000	1.00000000	1.00000000	1.00000000
2	2.03250000	2.03300000	2.03350000	2.03400000	2.03450000
3	3.09855625	3.10008900	3.10162225	3.10315600	3.10469025
4	4.19925933	4.20239194	4.20552660	4.20866330	4.21180206
5	5.33573526	5.34107087	5.34641174	5.35175786	5.35710923
6	6.50914665	6.51732621	6.52551653	6.53371762	6.54192950
7	7.72069392	7.73239797	7.74412133	7.75586402	7.76762607
8	8.97161647	8.98756711	9.00354940	9.01956340	9.03560917
9	10.26319401	10.28415682	10.30516830	10.32622855	10.34733769
10	11.59674781	11.62353400	11.65039144	11.67732033	11.70432084
11	12.97364212	13.00711062	13.04067955	13.07434922	13.10811991
12	14.39528548	14.43634527	14.47754232	14.51887709	14.56035004
13	15.86313226	15.91274466	15.96253999	16.01251891	16.06268212
14	17.37868406	17.43786524	17.49728508	17.55694455	17.61684465
15	18.94349129	19.01331479	19.08344413	19.15388067	19.22462579
16	20.55915476	20.64075418	20.72273950	20.80511261	20.88787538
17	22.22732729	22.32189907	22.41695128	22.51248644	22.60850708
18	23.94971543	24.05852174	24.16791915	24.27791098	24.38850058
19	25.72808118	25.85245295	25.97754444	26.10335995	26.22990385
20	27.56424382	27.70558390	27.84779218	27.99087419	28.13483553
21	29.46008174	29.61986817	29.78069321	29.94256391	30.10548736
22	31.41753440	31.59732382	31.77834644	31.96061109	32.14412667
23	33.43860426	33.64003550	33.84292104	34.04727186	34.25309904
24	35.52535890	35.75015668	35.97665890	36.20487911	36.43483096
25	37.67993307	37.92991185	38.18187697	38.43584500	38.69183263
26	39.90453089	40.18159894	40.46096985	40.74266373	41.02670085
27	42.20142815	42.50759170	42.81641234	43.12791429	43.44212203
28	44.57297456	44.91034223	45.25076215	45.59426338	45.94087524
29	47.02159623	47.39238352	47.76666268	48.14446833	48.52583544
30	49.54979811	49.95633218	50.36684588	50.78138026	51.19997676
31	52.16016655	52.60489114	53.05413522	53.50794719	53.96637596
32	54.85537196	55.34085255	55.83144875	56.32721739	56.82821593
33	57.63817155	58.16710068	58.70180228	59.24234278	59.78878938
34	60.51141213	61.08661500	61.66831266	62.25658244	62.85150261
35	63.47803302	64.10247330	64.73420113	65.37330624	66.01987945
36	66.54106909	67.21785492	67.90279687	68.59599865	69.29756529
37	69.70365384	70.43604413	71.17754057	71.92826261	72.68833129
38	72.96902259	73.76043359	74.56198818	75.37382353	76.19607872
39	76.34051582	77.19452790	78.05981478	78.93653353	79.82484344
40	79.82158259	80.74194732	81.67481858	82.62037568	83.57880054

i	3.50	3.55	3.60	3.65	3.70
Years					
1	1.00000000	1.00000000	1.00000000	1.00000000	1.00000000
2	2.03500000	2.03550000	2.03600000	2.03650000	2.03700000
3	3.10622500	3.10776025	3.10929600	3.11083225	3.11236900
4	4.21494288	4.21808574	4.22123066	4.22437763	4.22752665
5	5.36246588	5.36782778	5.37319496	5.37856741	5.38394514
6	6.55015218	6.55838567	6.56662998	6.57488512	6.58315111
7	7.77940751	7.79120836	7.80302866	7.81486843	7.82672770
8	9.05168677	9.06779626	9.08393769	9.10011113	9.11631663
9	10.36849581	10.38970302	10.41095945	10.43226518	10.45362034
10	11.73139316	11.75853748	11.78575399	11.81304286	11.84040429
11	13.14199192	13.17596556	13.21004113	13.24421893	13.27849925
12	14.60196164	14.64371234	14.68560261	14.72763292	14.76980372
13	16.11303030	16.16356413	16.21428430	16.26519152	16.31628646
14	17.67698636	17.73737065	17.79799854	17.85887101	17.91998906
15	19.29568088	19.36704731	19.43872649	19.51071980	19.58302866
16	20.97102971	21.05457749	21.13852064	21.22286107	21.30760072
17	22.70501575	22.80201499	22.89950738	22.99749550	23.09598194
18	24.49969130	24.61148653	24.72388965	24.83690409	24.95053327
19	26.35718050	26.48519430	26.61394968	26.74345109	26.87370301
20	28.27968181	28.42541869	28.57205186	28.71958705	28.86803002
21	30.26947068	30.43452106	30.60064573	30.76785198	30.93614713
22	32.32890215	32.51494656	32.70226898	32.89087858	33.08078457
23	34.46041373	34.66922716	34.87955066	35.09139564	35.30477360
24	36.66652821	36.89998472	37.13521448	37.37223158	37.61105022
25	38.94985669	39.20993418	39.47208221	39.73631804	40.00265908
26	41.31310168	41.60188684	41.89307717	42.18669365	42.48275747
27	43.75906024	44.07875383	44.40122794	44.72650796	45.05461949
28	46.29062734	46.64354959	46.99967215	47.35902550	47.72164042
29	48.91079930	49.29939560	49.69166035	50.08762994	50.48734111
30	51.62267728	52.04952414	52.48056012	52.91582843	53.35537273
31	54.42947098	54.89728225	55.36986028	55.84725617	56.32952152
32	57.33450247	57.84613577	58.36317525	58.88568102	59.41371382
33	60.34121005	60.89967359	61.46424956	62.03500837	62.61202123
34	63.45315240	64.06161200	64.67696255	65.29928618	65.92866602
35	66.67401274	67.33579923	68.00533320	68.68271012	69.36802666
36	70.00760318	70.72622010	71.45352519	72.18962904	72.93464365
37	73.45786930	74.23700091	75.02585210	75.82455050	76.63322546
38	77.02889472	77.87241444	78.72678278	79.59214660	80.46865480
39	80.72490604	81.63688516	82.56094696	83.49725995	84.44599503
40	84.55027775	85.53499458	86.53314105	87.54490994	88.57049685

i	3.75	3.80	3.85	3.90	3.95
Years					
1	1.00000000	1.00000000	1.00000000	1.00000000	1.00000000
2	2.03750000	2.03800000	2.03850000	2.03900000	2.03950000
3	3.11390625	3.11544400	3.11698225	3.11852100	3.12006025
4	4.23067773	4.23383087	4.23698607	4.24014332	4.24330263
5	5.38932815	5.39471645	5.40011003	5.40550891	5.41091308
6	6.59142796	6.59971567	6.60801427	6.61632376	6.62464415
7	7.83860650	7.85050487	7.86242282	7.87436038	7.88631759
8	9.13255425	9.14882405	9.16512609	9.18146044	9.19782714
9	10.47502503	10.49647936	10.51798345	10.53953739	10.56114131
10	11.86783847	11.89534558	11.92292581	11.95057935	11.97830639
11	13.31288241	13.34736871	13.38195846	13.41665195	13.45144950
12	14.81211550	14.85456872	14.89716386	14.93990137	14.98278175
13	16.36756983	16.41904233	16.47070466	16.52255753	16.57460163
14	17.98135370	18.04296594	18.10482679	18.16693727	18.22929839
15	19.65565447	19.72859865	19.80186263	19.87544782	19.94935568
16	21.39274151	21.47828540	21.56423434	21.65059029	21.73735523
17	23.19496932	23.29446024	23.39445736	23.49496331	23.59598076
18	25.06478067	25.17964973	25.29514397	25.41126688	25.52802200
19	27.00470994	27.13647642	27.26900701	27.40230629	27.53637887
20	29.01738656	29.16766253	29.31886378	29.47099623	29.62406584
21	31.10553856	31.27603370	31.44764003	31.62036509	31.79421644
22	33.27199626	33.46452298	33.65837418	33.85355932	34.05008799
23	35.51969612	35.73617486	35.95422158	36.17384814	36.39506646
24	37.85168472	38.09414950	38.33845911	38.58462822	38.83267159
25	40.27112290	40.54172718	40.81448979	41.08942872	41.36656211
26	42.78129001	43.08231281	43.38584765	43.69191644	44.00054132
27	45.38558838	45.71944070	46.05620278	46.39590118	46.73856270
28	48.08754794	48.45677945	48.82936659	49.20534132	49.58473593
29	50.89083099	51.29813707	51.70929720	52.12434963	52.54333300
30	53.79923715	54.24746628	54.70010514	55.15719927	55.61879465
31	56.81670855	57.30886999	57.80605919	58.30833004	58.81573704
32	59.94733512	60.48660705	61.03159247	61.58235491	62.13895865
33	63.19536019	63.78509812	64.38130878	64.98406675	65.59344752
34	66.56518619	67.20893185	67.85998917	68.51844536	69.18438870
35	70.06138067	70.76287126	71.47259875	72.19066473	72.91717205
36	73.68868245	74.45186037	75.22429380	76.00610065	76.79740034
37	77.45200804	78.28103106	79.12042911	79.97033858	80.83089766
38	81.35645834	82.25571024	83.16656563	84.08918178	85.02371812
39	85.40732553	86.38142723	87.36847841	88.36865987	89.38215498
40	89.61010024	90.66392147	91.73216483	92.81503761	93.91275010

i	4.00	4.05	4.10	4.15	4.20
Years					
1	1.00000000	1.00000000	1.00000000	1.00000000	1.00000000
2	2.04000000	2.04050000	2.04100000	2.04150000	2.04200000
3	3.12160000	3.12314025	3.12468100	3.12622225	3.12776400
4	4.24646400	4.24962743	4.25279292	4.25596047	4.25913009
5	5.41632256	5.42173734	5.42715743	5.43258283	5.43801355
6	6.63297546	6.64131770	6.64967089	6.65803502	6.66641012
7	7.89829448	7.91029107	7.92230739	7.93434347	7.94639935
8	9.21422626	9.23065786	9.24712199	9.26361873	9.28014812
9	10.58279531	10.60449950	10.62625400	10.64805891	10.66991434
10	12.00610712	12.03398173	12.06193041	12.08995335	12.11805074
11	13.48635141	13.52135799	13.55646956	13.59168641	13.62700887
12	15.02580546	15.06897299	15.11228481	15.15574140	15.19934325
13	16.62683768	16.67926640	16.73188849	16.78470467	16.83771566
14	18.29191119	18.35477669	18.41789591	18.48126991	18.54489972
15	20.02358764	20.09814514	20.17302965	20.24824261	20.32378551
16	21.82453114	21.91212002	22.00012386	22.08854468	22.17738450
17	23.69751239	23.79956088	23.90212894	24.00521929	24.10883465
18	25.64541288	25.76344310	25.88211623	26.00143589	26.12140570
19	27.67122940	27.80686254	27.94328299	28.08049548	28.21850474
20	29.77807858	29.93304047	30.08895760	30.24583604	30.40368194
21	31.96920172	32.14532861	32.32260486	32.50103823	32.68063658
22	34.24796979	34.44721442	34.64783166	34.84983132	35.05322332
23	36.61788858	36.84232661	37.06839275	37.29609932	37.52545870
24	39.08260412	39.33444083	39.58819686	39.84388744	40.10152797
25	41.64590829	41.92748569	42.21131293	42.49740877	42.78579214
26	44.31174462	44.62554886	44.94197676	45.26105123	45.58279541
27	47.08421440	47.43288359	47.78459780	48.13938486	48.49727282
28	49.96758298	50.35391537	50.74376631	51.13716933	51.53415827
29	52.96628630	53.39324895	53.82426073	54.25936186	54.69859292
30	56.08493775	56.55567553	57.03105542	57.51112538	57.99593383
31	59.32833526	59.84618039	60.36932870	60.89783708	61.43176305
32	62.70146867	63.26995069	63.84447117	64.42509732	65.01189709
33	66.20952742	66.83238370	67.46209449	68.09873886	68.74239677
34	69.85790851	70.53909523	71.22804036	71.92483652	72.62957744
35	73.65222486	74.39592859	75.14839002	75.90971724	76.68001969
36	77.59831385	78.40896370	79.22947401	80.05997050	80.90058052
37	81.70224640	82.58452673	83.47788244	84.38245928	85.29840490
38	85.97033626	86.92920006	87.90047563	88.88433134	89.88093790
39	90.40914971	91.44983266	92.50439513	93.57303109	94.65593729
40	95.02551570	96.15355089	97.29707533	98.45631188	99.63148666

i	4.25	4.30	4.35	4.40	4.45
Years					
1	1.00000000	1.00000000	1.00000000	1.00000000	1.00000000
2	2.04250000	2.04300000	2.04350000	2.04400000	2.04450000
3	3.12930625	3.13084900	3.13239225	3.13393600	3.13548025
4	4.26230177	4.26547551	4.26865131	4.27182918	4.27500912
5	5.44344959	5.44889095	5.45433764	5.45978967	5.46524703
6	6.67479620	6.68319326	6.69160133	6.70002041	6.70845052
7	7.95847504	7.97057058	7.98268599	7.99482131	8.00697657
8	9.29671023	9.31330511	9.32993283	9.34659345	9.36328703
9	10.69182041	10.71377723	10.73578491	10.75784356	10.77995330
10	12.14622278	12.17446965	12.20279155	12.23118868	12.25966122
11	13.66243725	13.69797185	13.73361299	13.76936098	13.80521614
12	15.24309083	15.28698463	15.33102515	15.37521286	15.41954826
13	16.89092219	16.94432497	16.99792474	17.05172223	17.10571816
14	18.60878638	18.67293095	18.73733447	18.80199801	18.86692262
15	20.39965980	20.47586698	20.55240852	20.62928592	20.70650067
16	22.26664534	22.35632926	22.44643829	22.53697450	22.62793995
17	24.21297777	24.31765142	24.42285836	24.52860138	24.63488328
18	26.24202933	26.36331043	26.48525269	26.60785984	26.73113559
19	28.35731557	28.49693278	28.63736119	28.77860567	28.92067112
20	30.56250149	30.72230089	30.88308640	31.04486432	31.20764099
21	32.86140780	33.04335982	33.22650066	33.41083835	33.59638101
22	35.25801763	35.46422430	35.67185344	35.88091524	36.09141997
23	37.75648338	37.98918594	38.22357906	38.45967551	38.69748815
24	40.36113392	40.62272094	40.88630475	41.15190123	41.41952638
25	43.07648211	43.36949794	43.66485901	43.96258489	44.26269530
26	45.90723260	46.23438635	46.56428037	46.89693862	47.23238524
27	48.85828999	49.22246496	49.58982657	49.96040392	50.33422639
28	51.93476732	52.33903095	52.74698402	53.15866169	53.57409946
29	55.14199493	55.58960929	56.04147783	56.49764281	56.95814689
30	58.48552971	58.97996248	59.47928212	59.98353909	60.49278442
31	61.97116472	62.51610087	63.06663089	63.62281481	64.18471333
32	65.60493922	66.20429321	66.81002933	67.42221866	68.04093307
33	69.39314914	70.05107782	70.71626561	71.38879628	72.06875459
34	73.34235798	74.06327416	74.79242316	75.52990332	76.27581417
35	77.45940819	78.24799495	79.04589357	79.85321906	80.67008790
36	81.75143304	82.61265874	83.48438994	84.36676070	85.25990682
37	86.22586895	87.16500306	88.11596090	89.07889817	90.05397267
38	90.89046838	91.91309819	92.94900520	93.99836969	95.06137445
39	95.75331328	96.86536141	97.99228693	99.13429796	100.29160562
40	100.82282910	102.03057196	103.25495141	104.49620707	105.75458207

i	4.50	4.55	4.60	4.65	4.70
Years					
1	1.00000000	1.00000000	1.00000000	1.00000000	1.00000000
2	2.04500000	2.04550000	2.04600000	2.04650000	2.04700000
3	3.13702500	3.13857025	3.14011600	3.14166225	3.14320900
4	4.27819112	4.28137520	4.28456134	4.28774954	4.29093982
5	5.47070973	5.47617777	5.48165116	5.48712990	5.49261399
6	6.71689166	6.72534386	6.73380711	6.74228144	6.75076685
7	8.01915179	8.03134700	8.04356224	8.05579753	8.06805289
8	9.38001362	9.39677329	9.41356610	9.43039211	9.44725138
9	10.80211423	10.82432647	10.84659014	10.86890534	10.89127220
10	12.28820937	12.31683333	12.34553329	12.37430944	12.40316199
11	13.84117879	13.87724925	13.91342782	13.94971483	13.98611060
12	15.46403184	15.50866409	15.55344550	15.59837657	15.64345780
13	17.15991327	17.21430830	17.26890399	17.32370108	17.37870032
14	18.93210937	18.99755933	19.06327358	19.12925318	19.19549923
15	20.78405429	20.86194828	20.94018416	21.01876345	21.09768770
16	22.71933673	22.81116693	22.90343263	22.99613596	23.08927902
17	24.74170689	24.84907502	24.95699053	25.06545628	25.17447513
18	26.85508370	26.97970794	27.10501210	27.23099999	27.35767546
19	29.06356246	29.20728465	29.35184265	29.49724149	29.64348621
20	31.37142277	31.53621610	31.70202742	31.86886322	32.03673006
21	33.78313680	33.97111393	34.16032068	34.35076536	34.54245637
22	36.30337795	36.51679961	36.73169543	36.94807595	37.16595182
23	38.93702996	39.17831400	39.42135342	39.66616148	39.91275156
24	41.68919631	41.96092728	42.23473567	42.51063799	42.78865088
25	44.56521015	44.87014947	45.17753352	45.48738266	45.79971747
26	47.57064460	47.91174128	48.25570006	48.60254595	48.95230420
27	50.71132361	51.09172550	51.47546226	51.86256434	52.25306249
28	53.99333317	54.41639901	54.84333352	55.27417358	55.70895643
29	57.42303316	57.89234517	58.36612687	58.84442265	59.32727738
30	61.00706966	61.52644687	62.05096870	62.58068831	63.11565942
31	64.75238779	65.32590021	65.90531326	66.49069031	67.08209541
32	68.66624524	69.29822867	69.93695767	70.58250741	71.23495390
33	72.75622628	73.45129807	74.15405772	74.86459401	75.58299673
34	77.03025646	77.79333213	78.56514438	79.34579763	80.13539758
35	81.49661800	82.33292875	83.17914102	84.03537722	84.90176126
36	86.16396581	87.07907700	88.00538151	88.94302226	89.89214404
37	91.04134427	92.04117501	93.05362906	94.07887280	95.11707481
38	96.13820476	97.22904847	98.33409599	99.45354038	100.58757733
39	101.46442398	102.65297018	103.85746441	105.07813001	106.31519346
40	107.03032306	108.32368032	109.63490777	110.96426305	112.31200755

i	4.75	4.80	4.85	4.90	4.95
Years					
1	1.00000000	1.00000000	1.00000000	1.00000000	1.00000000
2	2.04750000	2.04800000	2.04850000	2.04900000	2.04950000
3	3.14475625	3.14630400	3.14785225	3.14940100	3.15095025
4	4.29413217	4.29732659	4.30052308	4.30372165	4.30692229
5	5.49810345	5.50359827	5.50909845	5.51460401	5.52011494
6	6.75926336	6.76777099	6.77628973	6.78481961	6.79336063
7	8.08032837	8.09262399	8.10493978	8.11727577	8.12963198
8	9.46414397	9.48106994	9.49802936	9.51502228	9.53204876
9	10.91369081	10.93616130	10.95868378	10.98125837	11.00388518
10	12.43209112	12.46109704	12.49017995	12.51934003	12.54857749
11	14.02261545	14.05922970	14.09595367	14.13278769	14.16973208
12	15.68868969	15.73407273	15.77960743	15.82529429	15.87113382
13	17.43390245	17.48930822	17.54491839	17.60073371	17.65675494
14	19.26201281	19.32879501	19.39584693	19.46316966	19.53076431
15	21.17695842	21.25657717	21.33654551	21.41686498	21.49753715
16	23.18286395	23.27689288	23.37136796	23.46629136	23.56166523
17	25.28404998	25.39418374	25.50487931	25.61613964	25.72796766
18	27.48504236	27.61310456	27.74186596	27.87133048	28.00150206
19	29.79058187	29.93853357	30.08734645	30.23702567	30.38757641
20	32.20563451	32.37558319	32.54658276	32.71863993	32.89176145
21	34.73540215	34.92961118	35.12509202	35.32185329	35.51990364
22	37.38533375	37.60623252	37.82865898	38.05262410	38.27813887
23	40.16113710	40.41133168	40.66334895	40.91720268	41.17290674
24	43.06879111	43.35107560	43.63552137	43.92214561	44.21096563
25	46.11455869	46.43192723	46.75184416	47.07433074	47.39940843
26	49.30500023	49.66065973	50.01930860	50.38097295	50.74567914
27	52.64698774	53.04437140	53.44524506	53.84964062	54.25759026
28	56.14771966	56.59050123	57.03733945	57.48827302	57.94334098
29	59.81473634	60.30684529	60.80365041	61.30519839	61.81153636
30	63.65593632	64.20157386	64.75262746	65.30915311	65.87120741
31	67.67959329	68.28324940	68.89312989	69.50930162	70.13183217
32	71.89437398	72.56084538	73.23444669	73.91525740	74.60335787
33	76.30935674	77.04376595	77.78631735	78.53710501	79.29622408
34	80.93405119	81.74186672	82.55895375	83.38542315	84.22138717
35	85.77841862	86.66547632	87.56306300	88.47130889	89.39034584
36	90.85289350	91.82541919	92.80987156	93.80640302	94.81516796
37	96.16840594	97.23303931	98.31115033	99.40291677	100.50851877
38	101.73640522	102.90022519	104.07924112	105.27365969	106.48369045
39	107.56888447	108.83943600	110.12708431	111.43206902	112.75463313
40	113.67840648	115.06372893	116.46824790	117.89224040	119.33598747

i	5.00	5.05	5.10	5.15	5.20
Years					
1	1.00000000	1.00000000	1.00000000	1.00000000	1.00000000
2	2.05000000	2.05050000	2.05100000	2.05150000	2.05200000
3	3.15250000	3.15405025	3.15560100	3.15715225	3.15870400
4	4.31012500	4.31332979	4.31653665	4.31974559	4.32295661
5	5.52563125	5.53115294	5.53668002	5.54221249	5.54775035
6	6.80191281	6.81047617	6.81905070	6.82763643	6.83623337
7	8.14200845	8.15440521	8.16682229	8.17925971	8.19171751
8	9.54910888	9.56620268	9.58333022	9.60049158	9.61768682
9	11.02656432	11.04929591	11.07208007	11.09491690	11.11780653
10	12.57789254	12.60728535	12.63675615	12.66630512	12.69593247
11	14.20678716	14.24395326	14.28123071	14.31861983	14.35612096
12	15.91712652	15.96327290	16.00957348	16.05602876	16.10263925
13	17.71298285	17.76941819	17.82606173	17.88291424	17.93997649
14	19.59863199	19.66677380	19.73519087	19.80388432	19.87285527
15	21.57856359	21.65994588	21.74168561	21.82378436	21.90624374
16	23.65749177	23.75377315	23.85051157	23.94770926	24.04536841
17	25.84036636	25.95333869	26.06688766	26.18101628	26.29572757
18	28.13238467	28.26398230	28.39629894	28.52933862	28.66310541
19	30.53900391	30.69131340	30.84451018	30.99859956	31.15358689
20	33.06595410	33.24122473	33.41758020	33.59502744	33.77357340
21	35.71925181	35.91990658	36.12187679	36.32517135	36.52979922
22	38.50521440	38.73386186	38.96409251	39.19591768	39.42934878
23	41.43047512	41.68992188	41.95126122	42.21450744	42.47967492
24	44.50199887	44.79526294	45.09077555	45.38855457	45.68861801
25	47.72709882	48.05742372	48.39040510	48.72606513	49.06442615
26	51.11345376	51.48432361	51.85831576	52.23545748	52.61577631
27	54.66912645	55.08428196	55.50308986	55.92558354	56.35179668
28	58.40258277	58.86603820	59.33374745	59.80575110	60.28209011
29	62.32271191	62.83877312	63.35976857	63.88574728	64.41675879
30	66.43884750	67.01213117	67.59111676	68.17586326	68.76643025
31	70.76078988	71.39624379	72.03826372	72.68692022	73.34228462
32	75.29882937	76.00175410	76.71221517	77.43029661	78.15608342
33	80.06377084	80.83984269	81.62453814	82.41795689	83.22019976
34	85.06695938	85.92225474	86.78738959	87.66248167	88.54765015
35	90.32030735	91.26132861	92.21354646	93.17709947	94.15212795
36	95.83632272	96.87002570	97.91643733	98.97572010	100.04803861
37	101.62813886	102.76196200	103.91017563	105.07296968	106.25053662
38	107.70954580	108.95144108	110.20959459	111.48422762	112.77556452
39	114.09502309	115.45348885	116.83028391	118.22566534	119.63989387
40	120.79977424	122.28389004	123.78862839	125.31428711	126.86116836

i	5.25	5.30	5.35	5.40	5.45
Years					
1	1.00000000	1.00000000	1.00000000	1.00000000	1.00000000
2	2.05250000	2.05300000	2.05350000	2.05400000	2.05450000
3	3.16025625	3.16180900	3.16336225	3.16491600	3.16647025
4	4.32616970	4.32938488	4.33260213	4.33582146	4.33904288
5	5.55329361	5.55884228	5.56439634	5.56995582	5.57552072
6	6.84484153	6.85346092	6.86209155	6.87073344	6.87938659
7	8.20419571	8.21669434	8.22921345	8.24175304	8.25431316
8	9.63491598	9.65217914	9.66947637	9.68680771	9.70417323
9	11.14074907	11.16374464	11.18679335	11.20989532	11.23305067
10	12.72563840	12.75542311	12.78528680	12.81522967	12.84525193
11	14.39373441	14.43146053	14.46929964	14.50725207	14.54531816
12	16.14940547	16.19632794	16.24340717	16.29064369	16.33803800
13	17.99724926	18.05473332	18.11242945	18.17033844	18.22846108
14	19.94210484	20.01163418	20.08144443	20.15153672	20.22191220
15	21.98906535	22.07225080	22.15580171	22.23971970	22.32400642
16	24.14349128	24.24208009	24.34113710	24.44066457	24.54066477
17	26.41102457	26.52691033	26.64338793	26.76046045	26.87813100
18	28.79760336	28.93283658	29.06880919	29.20552532	29.34298914
19	31.30947754	31.46627692	31.62399048	31.78262369	31.94218205
20	33.95322511	34.13398960	34.31587397	34.49888536	34.68303097
21	36.73576943	36.94309105	37.15177323	37.36182517	37.57325616
22	39.66439732	39.90107487	40.13939309	40.37936373	40.62099862
23	42.74677818	43.01583184	43.28685062	43.55984938	43.83484304
24	45.99098403	46.29567093	46.60269713	46.91208124	47.22384199
25	49.40551070	49.74934149	50.09594143	50.44533363	50.79754138
26	52.99930001	53.38605658	53.77607430	54.16938164	54.56600738
27	56.78176326	57.21551758	57.65309427	58.09452825	58.53985478
28	60.76280583	61.24794002	61.73753481	62.23163278	62.73027687
29	64.95285313	65.49408084	66.04049293	66.59214095	67.14907696
30	69.36287792	69.96526712	70.57365930	71.18811656	71.80870165
31	74.00442901	74.67342628	75.34935007	76.03227485	76.72227589
32	78.88966154	79.63111787	80.38054030	81.13801770	81.90363993
33	84.03136877	84.85156712	85.68089921	86.51947065	87.36738830
34	89.44301563	90.34870017	91.26482731	92.19152207	93.12891097
35	95.13877395	96.13718128	97.14749557	98.16986426	99.20443661
36	101.13355958	102.23245189	103.34488659	104.47103693	105.61107841
37	107.44307146	108.65077184	109.87383802	111.11247292	112.36688218
38	114.08383271	115.40926275	116.75208835	118.11254646	119.49087726
39	121.07323393	122.52595368	123.99832508	125.49062397	127.00313007
40	128.42957871	130.01982922	131.63223547	133.26711766	134.92480066

i	5.50	5.55	5.60	5.65	5.70
Years					
1	1.00000000	1.00000000	1.00000000	1.00000000	1.00000000
2	2.05500000	2.05550000	2.05600000	2.05650000	2.05700000
3	3.16802500	3.16958025	3.17113600	3.17269225	3.17424900
4	4.34226638	4.34549195	4.34871962	4.35194936	4.35518119
5	5.58109103	5.58666676	5.59224791	5.59783450	5.60342652
6	6.88805103	6.89672676	6.90541380	6.91411215	6.92282183
7	8.26689384	8.27949510	8.29211697	8.30475949	8.31742268
8	9.72157300	9.73900708	9.75647552	9.77397840	9.79151577
9	11.25625951	11.27952197	11.30283815	11.32620818	11.34963217
10	12.87535379	12.90553544	12.93579709	12.96613894	12.99656120
11	14.58349825	14.62179265	14.66020172	14.69872579	14.73736519
12	16.38559065	16.43330215	16.48117302	16.52920380	16.57739501
13	18.28679814	18.34535042	18.40411871	18.46310381	18.52230652
14	20.29257203	20.36351736	20.43474936	20.50626918	20.57807799
15	22.40866350	22.49369258	22.57909532	22.66487338	22.75102844
16	24.64113999	24.74209252	24.84352466	24.94543873	25.04783706
17	26.99640269	27.11527865	27.23476204	27.35485602	27.47556377
18	29.48120483	29.62017662	29.75990871	29.90040538	30.04167091
19	32.10267110	32.26409642	32.42646360	32.58977829	32.75404615
20	34.86831801	35.05475377	35.24234556	35.43110076	35.62102678
21	37.78607550	38.00029260	38.21591691	38.43295796	38.65142531
22	40.86430965	41.10930884	41.35600826	41.60442008	41.85455655
23	44.11184669	44.39087548	44.67194472	44.95506981	45.24026627
24	47.53799825	47.85456907	48.17357363	48.49503126	48.81896145
25	51.15258816	51.51049766	51.87129375	52.23500052	52.60164225
26	54.96598051	55.36933028	55.77608620	56.18627805	56.59993586
27	58.98910943	59.44232811	59.89954703	60.36080276	60.82613221
28	63.23351045	63.74137732	64.25392166	64.77118812	65.29322174
29	67.71135353	68.27902376	68.85214128	69.43076025	70.01493538
30	72.43547797	73.06850958	73.70786119	74.35359820	75.00578670
31	77.41942926	78.12381186	78.83550141	79.55457650	80.28111654
32	82.67749787	83.45968341	84.25028949	85.04941007	85.85714018
33	88.22476025	89.09169584	89.96830571	90.85470174	91.75099717
34	94.07712207	95.03628496	96.00653082	96.98799239	97.98080401
35	100.25136378	101.31079878	102.38289655	103.46781396	104.56570984
36	106.76518879	107.93354811	109.11633876	110.31374545	111.52595530
37	113.63727417	114.92386003	116.22685373	117.54647207	118.88293475
38	120.88732425	122.30213426	123.73555754	125.18784774	126.65926203
39	128.53612708	130.08990271	131.66474876	133.26096114	134.87883997
40	136.60561407	138.30989232	140.03797469	141.79020544	143.56693385

i	5.75	5.80	5.85	5.90	5.95
Years					
1	1.00000000	1.00000000	1.00000000	1.00000000	1.00000000
2	2.05750000	2.05800000	2.05850000	2.05900000	2.05950000
3	3.17580625	3.17736400	3.17892225	3.18048100	3.18204025
4	4.35841511	4.36165111	4.36488920	4.36812938	4.37137164
5	5.60902398	5.61462688	5.62023522	5.62584901	5.63146826
6	6.93154286	6.94027524	6.94901898	6.95777410	6.96654062
7	8.33010657	8.34281120	8.35553659	8.36828278	8.38104979
8	9.80908770	9.82669425	9.84433548	9.86201146	9.87972225
9	11.37311024	11.39664251	11.42022911	11.44387014	11.46756572
10	13.02706408	13.05764778	13.08831251	13.11905847	13.14988588
11	14.77612027	14.81499135	14.85397879	14.89308292	14.93230409
12	16.62574718	16.67426085	16.72293655	16.77177482	16.82077619
13	18.58172764	18.64136798	18.70122834	18.76130953	18.82161237
14	20.65017698	20.72256732	20.79525020	20.86822679	20.94149830
15	22.83756216	22.92447623	23.01177233	23.09945217	23.18751745
16	25.15072198	25.25409585	25.35796101	25.46231985	25.56717474
17	27.59688850	27.71883341	27.84140173	27.96459672	28.08842164
18	30.18370959	30.32652575	30.47012374	30.61450793	30.75968273
19	32.91927289	33.08546424	33.25262597	33.42076390	33.58988385
20	35.81213108	36.00442116	36.19790459	36.39258897	36.58848194
21	38.87132862	39.09267759	39.31548201	39.53975172	39.76549661
22	42.10643001	42.36005289	42.61543771	42.87259707	43.13154366
23	45.52754974	45.81693596	46.10844082	46.40208030	46.69787051
24	49.14538385	49.47431825	49.80578460	50.13980303	50.47639381
25	52.97124342	53.34382870	53.71942300	54.09805141	54.47973924
26	57.01708991	57.43777077	57.86200925	58.28983645	58.72128372
27	61.29557258	61.76916147	62.24693679	62.72893680	63.21520010
28	65.82006801	66.35177284	66.88838259	67.42994407	67.97650451
29	70.60472192	71.20017566	71.80135297	72.40831077	73.02110653
30	75.66449343	76.32978585	77.00173212	77.68040110	78.36586237
31	81.01520180	81.75691343	82.50633345	83.26354477	84.02863118
32	86.67357590	87.49881441	88.33295396	89.17609391	90.02833473
33	92.65730652	93.57374565	94.50043177	95.43748345	96.38502065
34	98.98510164	100.00102289	101.02870702	102.06829497	103.11992938
35	105.67674499	106.80108222	107.93888638	109.09032438	110.25556518
36	112.75315782	113.99554499	115.25331124	116.52665351	117.81577130
37	120.23646440	121.60728660	122.99562995	124.40172607	125.82580970
38	128.15006110	129.66050922	131.19087430	132.74142791	134.31244537
39	136.51868962	138.18081876	139.86554044	141.57317216	143.30403587
40	145.36851427	147.19530625	149.04767456	150.92598931	152.83062601

i	6.00	6.05	6.10	6.15	6.20
Years					
1	1.00000000	1.00000000	1.00000000	1.00000000	1.00000000
2	2.06000000	2.06050000	2.06100000	2.06150000	2.06200000
3	3.18360000	3.18516025	3.18672100	3.18828225	3.18984400
4	4.37461600	4.37786245	4.38111098	4.38436161	4.38761433
5	5.63709296	5.64272312	5.64835875	5.65399985	5.65964642
6	6.97531854	6.98410787	6.99290863	7.00172084	7.01054449
7	8.39383765	8.40664640	8.41947606	8.43232667	8.44519825
8	9.89746791	9.91524851	9.93306410	9.95091476	9.96880054
9	11.49131598	11.51512104	11.53898101	11.56289602	11.58686618
10	13.18079494	13.21178586	13.24285885	13.27401412	13.30525188
11	14.97164264	15.01109891	15.05067324	15.09036599	15.13017750
12	16.86994120	16.91927039	16.96876431	17.01842350	17.06824850
13	18.88213767	18.94288625	19.00385893	19.06505654	19.12647991
14	21.01506593	21.08893087	21.16309433	21.23755752	21.31232166
15	23.27596988	23.36481119	23.45404308	23.54366731	23.63368561
16	25.67252808	25.77838226	25.88473971	25.99160285	26.09897412
17	28.21287976	28.33797439	28.46370883	28.59008642	28.71711051
18	30.90565255	31.05242184	31.19999507	31.34837674	31.49757136
19	33.75999170	33.93109336	34.10319477	34.27630191	34.45042079
20	36.78559120	36.98392451	37.18348965	37.38429448	37.58634688
21	39.99272668	40.22145194	40.45168252	40.68342859	40.91670038
22	43.39229028	43.65484979	43.91923516	44.18545944	44.45353581
23	46.99582769	47.29596820	47.59830850	47.90286520	48.20965503
24	50.81557735	51.15737427	51.50180532	51.84889141	52.19865364
25	54.86451200	55.25239542	55.64341544	56.03759823	56.43497016
26	59.15638272	59.59516534	60.03766378	60.48391052	60.93393831
27	63.70576568	64.20067284	64.69996128	65.20367102	65.71184249
28	68.52811162	69.08481355	69.64665891	70.21369679	70.78597672
29	73.63979832	74.26444477	74.89510511	75.53183914	76.17470728
30	79.05818622	79.75744368	80.46370652	81.17704725	81.89753913
31	84.80167739	85.58276902	86.37199262	87.16943565	87.97518656
32	90.88977803	91.76052655	92.64068417	93.53035595	94.42964812
33	97.34316471	98.31203840	99.29176590	100.28247284	101.28428631
34	104.18375460	105.25991672	106.34856362	107.44984492	108.56391206
35	111.43477987	112.62814169	113.83582600	115.05801038	116.29487460
36	119.12086666	120.44214426	121.77981139	123.13407802	124.50515683
37	127.26811866	128.72889399	130.20837988	131.70682382	133.22447655
38	135.90420578	137.51699207	139.15109105	140.80679348	142.48439410
39	145.05845813	146.83677009	148.63930761	150.46641128	152.31842653
40	154.76196562	156.72039468	158.70630537	160.72009557	162.76216898

i	6.25	6.30	6.35	6.40	6.45
Years					
1	1.00000000	1.00000000	1.00000000	1.00000000	1.00000000
2	2.06250000	2.06300000	2.06350000	2.06400000	2.06450000
3	3.19140625	3.19296900	3.19453225	3.19609600	3.19766025
4	4.39086914	4.39412605	4.39738505	4.40064614	4.40390934
5	5.66529846	5.67095599	5.67661900	5.68228750	5.68796149
6	7.01937962	7.02822622	7.03708430	7.04595390	7.05483500
7	8.45809084	8.47100447	8.48393916	8.49689495	8.50987186
8	9.98672152	10.00467775	10.02266929	10.04069622	10.05875860
9	11.61089161	11.63497245	11.65910879	11.68330078	11.70754853
10	13.33657234	13.36797571	13.39946220	13.43103203	13.46268541
11	15.17010811	15.21015818	15.25032805	15.29061808	15.33102862
12	17.11823987	17.16839815	17.21872388	17.26921764	17.31987996
13	19.18812986	19.25000723	19.31211285	19.37444757	19.43701222
14	21.38738798	21.46275768	21.53843202	21.61441221	21.69069951
15	23.72409973	23.81491142	23.90612245	23.99773459	24.08974962
16	26.20685596	26.31525084	26.42416123	26.53358961	26.64353848
17	28.84478446	28.97311164	29.10209546	29.23173934	29.36204671
18	31.64758348	31.79841767	31.95007853	32.10257066	32.25589872
19	34.62555745	34.80171799	34.97890851	35.15713518	35.33640419
20	37.78965479	37.99422622	38.20006920	38.40719183	38.61560226
21	41.15150822	41.38786247	41.62577360	41.86525211	42.10630860
22	44.72347748	44.99529781	45.26901022	45.54462825	45.82216551
23	48.51869482	48.83000157	49.14359237	49.45948445	49.77769518
24	52.55111325	52.90629167	53.26421049	53.62489146	53.98835652
25	56.83555783	57.23938804	57.64648785	58.05688451	58.47060552
26	61.38778019	61.84546949	62.30703983	62.77252512	63.24195957
27	66.22451645	66.74173407	67.26353686	67.78996673	68.32106597
28	71.36354873	71.94646331	72.53477145	73.12852460	73.72777472
29	76.82377053	77.47909050	78.14072944	78.80875017	79.48321619
30	82.62525619	83.36027321	84.10266576	84.85251019	85.60988364
31	88.78933470	89.61197042	90.44318503	91.28307084	92.13172113
32	95.33866812	96.25752455	97.18632728	98.12518737	99.07421714
33	102.29733487	103.32174860	104.35765906	105.40519936	106.46450415
34	109.69091830	110.83101876	111.98437041	113.15113212	114.33146467
35	117.54660070	118.81337294	120.09537793	121.39280458	122.70584414
36	125.89326324	127.29861544	128.72143443	130.16194407	131.62037108
37	134.76159219	136.31842821	137.89524552	139.49230849	141.10988502
38	144.18419170	145.90648919	147.65159361	149.41981623	151.21147260
39	154.19570369	156.09859801	158.02746980	159.98268447	161.96461259
40	164.83293517	166.93280968	169.06221414	171.22157628	173.41133010

i	6.50	6.55	6.60	6.65	6.70
Years					
1	1.00000000	1.00000000	1.00000000	1.00000000	1.00000000
2	2.06500000	2.06550000	2.06600000	2.06650000	2.06700000
3	3.19922500	3.20079025	3.20235600	3.20392225	3.20548900
4	4.40717463	4.41044201	4.41371150	4.41698308	4.42025676
5	5.69364098	5.69932596	5.70501645	5.71071245	5.71641397
6	7.06372764	7.07263181	7.08154754	7.09047483	7.09941370
7	8.52286994	8.53588920	8.54892968	8.56199141	8.57507442
8	10.07685648	10.09498994	10.11315904	10.13136384	10.14960441
9	11.73185215	11.75621178	11.78062753	11.80509953	11.82962790
10	13.49442254	13.52624365	13.55814895	13.59013865	13.62221297
11	15.37156001	15.41221261	15.45298678	15.49388287	15.53490124
12	17.37071141	17.42171254	17.47288391	17.52422608	17.57573962
13	19.49980765	19.56283471	19.62609425	19.68958712	19.75331418
14	21.76729515	21.84420038	21.92141647	21.99894466	22.07678623
15	24.18216933	24.27499551	24.36822995	24.46187448	24.55593090
16	26.75401034	26.86500771	26.97653313	27.08858913	27.20117828
17	29.49302101	29.62466572	29.75698432	29.88998031	30.02365722
18	32.41006738	32.56508132	32.72094528	32.87766400	33.03524225
19	35.51672176	35.69809415	35.88052767	36.06402866	36.24860348
20	38.82530867	39.03631932	39.24864250	39.46228656	39.67725992
21	42.34895373	42.59319823	42.83905290	43.08652862	43.33563633
22	46.10163573	46.38305272	46.66643039	46.95178277	47.23912397
23	50.09824205	50.42114267	50.74641480	51.07407633	51.40414527
24	54.35462778	54.72372751	55.09567818	55.47050240	55.84822301
25	58.88767859	59.30813167	59.73199294	60.15929081	60.59005395
26	63.71537769	64.19281429	64.67430447	65.15988365	65.64958756
27	68.85687725	69.39744363	69.94280857	70.49301592	71.04810993
28	74.33257427	74.94297618	75.55903393	76.18080147	76.80833329
29	80.16419159	80.85174112	81.54593017	82.24682477	82.95449162
30	86.37486405	87.14753017	87.92796156	88.71623862	89.51244256
31	92.98923021	93.85569339	94.73120703	95.61586849	96.50977621
32	100.03353017	101.00324131	101.98346669	102.97432374	103.97593122
33	107.53570963	108.61895362	109.71437549	110.82211627	111.94231861
34	115.52553076	116.73349508	117.95552427	119.19178700	120.44245396
35	124.03469026	125.37953901	126.74058887	128.11804084	129.51209837
36	133.09694513	134.59189881	136.10546774	137.63789056	139.18940897
37	142.74824656	144.40766818	146.08842861	147.79081028	149.51509937
38	153.02688259	154.86637045	156.73026490	158.61889916	160.53261102
39	163.97362996	166.01011771	168.07446238	170.16705595	172.28829596
40	175.63191590	177.88378042	180.16737690	182.48316518	184.83161179

i	6.75	6.80	6.85	6.90	6.95
Years					
1	1.00000000	1.00000000	1.00000000	1.00000000	1.00000000
2	2.06750000	2.06800000	2.06850000	2.06900000	2.06950000
3	3.20705625	3.20862400	3.21019225	3.21176100	3.21333025
4	4.42353255	4.42681043	4.43009042	4.43337251	4.43665670
5	5.72212099	5.72783354	5.73355161	5.73927521	5.74500434
6	7.10836416	7.11732622	7.12629990	7.13528520	7.14428215
7	8.58817874	8.60130441	8.61445144	8.62761988	8.64080975
8	10.16788081	10.18619310	10.20454137	10.22292565	10.24134603
9	11.85421276	11.87885424	11.90355245	11.92830752	11.95311958
10	13.65437212	13.68661632	13.71894579	13.75136074	13.78386139
11	15.57604224	15.61730623	15.65869358	15.70020463	15.74183976
12	17.62742509	17.67928306	17.73131409	17.78351875	17.83589762
13	19.81727629	19.88147431	19.94590910	20.01058155	20.07549251
14	22.15494244	22.23341456	22.31220388	22.39131167	22.47073924
15	24.65040105	24.74528675	24.84058984	24.93631218	25.03245561
16	27.31430312	27.42796625	27.54217025	27.65691772	27.77221128
17	30.15801858	30.29306795	30.42880891	30.56524504	30.70237996
18	33.19368484	33.35299657	33.51318232	33.67424695	33.83619537
19	36.43425856	36.62100034	36.80883531	36.99776999	37.18781095
20	39.89357101	40.11122836	40.33024053	40.55061612	40.77236381
21	43.58638706	43.83879189	44.09286200	44.34860863	44.60604309
22	47.52846818	47.81982974	48.11322305	48.40866263	48.70616309
23	51.73663979	52.07157816	52.40897883	52.74886035	53.09124142
24	56.22886297	56.61244548	56.99899388	57.38853171	57.78108270
25	61.02431122	61.46209177	61.90342496	62.34834040	62.79686795
26	66.14345223	66.64151401	67.14380957	67.65037589	68.16125027
27	71.60813526	72.17313696	72.74316052	73.31825182	73.89845717
28	77.44168439	78.08091028	78.72606702	79.37721120	80.03439994
29	83.66899808	84.39041218	85.11880261	85.85423877	86.59679073
30	90.31665545	91.12896020	91.94944059	92.77818125	93.61526769
31	97.41302970	98.32572950	99.24797727	100.17987575	101.12152879
32	104.98840920	106.01187910	107.04646371	108.09228718	109.14947505
33	113.07512682	114.22068688	115.37914648	116.55065499	117.73536356
34	121.70769788	122.98769359	124.28261801	125.59265019	126.91797133
35	130.92296749	132.35085676	133.79597734	135.25854305	136.73877034
36	140.76026779	142.35071501	143.96100179	145.59138252	147.24211488
37	151.26158587	153.03056364	154.82233041	156.63718792	158.47544186
38	162.47174292	164.43664196	166.42766005	168.44515388	170.48948507
39	174.43858556	176.61833362	178.82795476	181.06786950	183.33850428
40	187.21319009	189.62838030	192.07766966	194.56155250	197.08053033

i	7.00	7.05	7.10	7.15	7.20
Years					
1	1.00000000	1.00000000	1.00000000	1.00000000	1.00000000
2	2.07000000	2.07050000	2.07100000	2.07150000	2.07200000
3	3.21490000	3.21647025	3.21804100	3.21961225	3.22118400
4	4.43994300	4.44323140	4.44652191	4.44981453	4.45310925
5	5.75073901	5.75647922	5.76222497	5.76797626	5.77373311
6	7.15329074	7.16231100	7.17134294	7.18038657	7.18944190
7	8.65402109	8.66725393	8.68050829	8.69378421	8.70708171
8	10.25980257	10.27829533	10.29682438	10.31538978	10.33399160
9	11.97798875	12.00291515	12.02789891	12.05294015	12.07803899
10	13.81644796	13.84912067	13.88187973	13.91472537	13.94765780
11	15.78359932	15.82548367	15.86749319	15.90962823	15.95188916
12	17.88845127	17.94118027	17.99408521	18.04716665	18.10042518
13	20.14064286	20.20603348	20.27166526	20.33753907	20.40365580
14	22.55048786	22.63055884	22.71095349	22.79167311	22.87271901
15	25.12902201	25.22601324	25.32343119	25.42127774	25.51955478
16	27.88805355	28.00444718	28.12139480	28.23889909	28.35696273
17	30.84021730	30.97876070	31.11801383	31.25798038	31.39866404
18	33.99903251	34.16276333	34.32739281	34.49292598	34.65936785
19	37.37896479	37.57123815	37.76463770	37.95917018	38.15484234
20	40.99549232	41.22001043	41.44592698	41.67325085	41.90199099
21	44.86517678	45.12602117	45.38858780	45.65288829	45.91893434
22	49.00573916	49.30740566	49.61117753	49.91706980	50.22509761
23	53.43614090	53.78357776	54.13357114	54.48614029	54.84130464
24	58.17667076	58.57531999	58.97705469	59.38189932	59.78987857
25	63.24903772	63.70488005	64.16442557	64.62770512	65.09474983
26	68.67647036	69.19607410	69.72009978	70.24858604	70.78157182
27	74.48382328	75.07439732	75.67022687	76.27135994	76.87784499
28	80.69769091	81.36714233	82.04281298	82.72476218	83.41304983
29	87.34652927	88.10352587	88.86785270	89.63958267	90.41878941
30	94.46078632	95.31482444	96.17747024	97.04881283	97.92894225
31	102.07304137	103.03451956	104.00607063	104.98780295	105.97982609
32	110.21815426	111.29845319	112.39050164	113.49443086	114.61037357
33	118.93342506	120.14499414	121.37022726	122.60928267	123.86232047
34	128.25876481	129.61521623	130.98751339	132.37584638	133.78040754
35	138.23687835	139.75308897	141.28762684	142.84071939	144.41259689
36	148.91345984	150.60568175	152.31904835	154.05383083	155.81030386
37	160.33740202	162.22338231	164.13370078	166.06867974	168.02864574
38	172.56102017	174.66013076	176.78719354	178.94259034	181.12670823
39	185.64029158	187.97366998	190.33908428	192.73698555	195.16783123
40	199.63511199	202.22581372	204.85315926	207.51768001	210.21991508

i	7.25	7.30	7.35	7.40	7.45
Years					
1	1.00000000	1.00000000	1.00000000	1.00000000	1.00000000
2	2.07250000	2.07300000	2.07350000	2.07400000	2.07450000
3	3.22275625	3.22432900	3.22590225	3.22747600	3.22905025
4	4.45640608	4.45970502	4.46300607	4.46630922	4.46961449
5	5.77949552	5.78526348	5.79103701	5.79681611	5.80260077
6	7.19850894	7.20758772	7.21667823	7.22578050	7.23489453
7	8.72040084	8.73374162	8.74710408	8.76048826	8.77389417
8	10.35262990	10.37130476	10.39001623	10.40876439	10.42754929
9	12.10319557	12.12841001	12.15368242	12.17901295	12.20440171
10	13.98067725	14.01378394	14.04697808	14.08025991	14.11362964
11	15.99427635	16.03679016	16.07943097	16.12219914	16.16509505
12	18.15386139	18.20747585	18.26126915	18.31524188	18.36939463
13	20.47001634	20.53662158	20.60347243	20.67056978	20.73791453
14	22.95409252	23.03579496	23.11782765	23.20019194	23.28288916
15	25.61826423	25.71740799	25.81698799	25.91700615	26.01746440
16	28.47558839	28.59477877	28.71453660	28.83486460	28.95576550
17	31.54006854	31.68219762	31.82505504	31.96864458	32.11297003
18	34.82672351	34.99499805	35.16419659	35.33432428	35.50538630
19	38.35166097	38.54963291	38.74876504	38.94906428	39.15053758
20	42.13215639	42.36375611	42.59679927	42.83129503	43.06725263
21	46.18673773	46.45631031	46.72766402	47.00081086	47.27576295
22	50.53527621	50.84762096	51.16214732	51.47887087	51.79780729
23	55.19908374	55.55949729	55.92256515	56.28830731	56.65674393
24	60.20101731	60.61534059	61.03287369	61.45364205	61.87767135
25	65.56559106	66.04026046	66.51878990	67.00121157	67.48755787
26	71.31909641	71.86119947	72.40792096	72.95930122	73.51538093
27	77.48973090	78.10706703	78.72990315	79.35828951	79.99227681
28	84.10773639	84.80888292	85.51655103	86.23080294	86.95170143
29	91.20554728	91.99993138	92.80201754	93.61188235	94.42960319
30	98.81794946	99.71592637	100.62296582	101.53916165	102.46460862
31	106.98225080	107.99518899	109.01875381	110.05305961	111.09822197
32	115.73846398	116.87883779	118.03163222	119.19698602	120.37503950
33	125.12950262	126.41099295	127.70695719	129.01756299	130.34297995
34	135.20139156	136.63899543	138.09341854	139.56486265	141.05353195
35	146.00349245	147.61364210	149.24328480	150.89266248	152.56202008
36	157.58874565	159.38943797	161.21266623	163.05871951	164.92789058
37	170.01392971	172.02486694	174.06179720	176.12506475	178.21501843
38	183.33993961	185.58268223	187.85533930	190.15831954	192.49203730
39	197.63208523	200.13021803	202.66270674	205.23003519	207.83269408
40	212.96041141	215.73972395	218.55841568	221.41705779	224.31622979

i	7.50	7.55	7.60	7.65	7.70
Years					
1	1.00000000	1.00000000	1.00000000	1.00000000	1.00000000
2	2.07500000	2.07550000	2.07600000	2.07650000	2.07700000
3	3.23062500	3.23220025	3.23377600	3.23535225	3.23692900
4	4.47292188	4.47623137	4.47954298	4.48285670	4.48617253
5	5.80839102	5.81418684	5.81998824	5.82579523	5.83160782
6	7.24402034	7.25315794	7.26230735	7.27146857	7.28064162
7	8.78732187	8.80077137	8.81424271	8.82773592	8.84125102
8	10.44637101	10.46522961	10.48412515	10.50305771	10.52202735
9	12.22984883	12.25535444	12.28091866	12.30654163	12.33222346
10	14.14708750	14.18063370	14.21426848	14.24799206	14.28180467
11	16.20811906	16.25127155	16.29455289	16.33796346	16.38150363
12	18.42372799	18.47824255	18.53293891	18.58781766	18.64287940
13	20.80550759	20.87334986	20.94144226	21.00978571	21.07838112
14	23.36592066	23.44928778	23.53299188	23.61703432	23.70141647
15	26.11836470	26.21970900	26.32149926	26.42373744	26.52642553
16	29.07724206	29.19929703	29.32193320	29.44515336	29.56896030
17	32.25803521	32.40384396	32.55040013	32.69770759	32.84577024
18	35.67738785	35.85033418	36.02423054	36.19908222	36.37489455
19	39.35319194	39.55703441	39.76207206	39.96831201	40.17576143
20	43.30468134	43.54359050	43.78398953	44.02588788	44.26929506
21	47.55253244	47.83113159	48.11157274	48.39386830	48.67803078
22	52.11897237	52.44238202	52.76805226	53.09599923	53.42623915
23	57.02789530	57.40178187	57.77842424	58.15784317	58.54005957
24	62.30498744	62.73561640	63.16958448	63.60691817	64.04764415
25	67.97786150	68.47215543	68.97047290	69.47284741	69.97931275
26	74.07620112	74.64180317	75.21222884	75.78752024	76.36771983
27	80.63191620	81.27725931	81.92835823	82.58526553	83.24803426
28	87.67930991	88.41369239	89.15491346	89.90303835	90.65813290
29	95.25525816	96.08892616	96.93068688	97.78062078	98.63880913
30	103.39940252	104.34364009	105.29741908	106.26083827	107.23399744
31	112.15435771	113.22158491	114.30002293	115.38979240	116.49101524
32	121.56593454	122.76981457	123.98682468	125.21711152	126.46082341
33	131.68337963	133.03893558	134.40982335	135.79622055	137.19830681
34	142.55963310	144.08337521	145.62496993	147.18463142	148.76257644
35	154.25160558	155.96167004	157.69246764	159.44425572	161.21729482
36	166.82047600	168.73677613	170.67709518	172.64174129	174.63102653
37	180.33201170	182.47640272	184.64855441	186.84883449	189.07761557
38	194.85691258	197.25337113	199.68184455	202.14277033	204.63659197
39	210.47118102	213.14600065	215.85766474	218.60669226	221.39360955
40	227.25651960	230.23852370	233.26284726	236.33010422	239.44091748

i	7.75	7.80	7.85	7.90	7.95
Years					
1	1.00000000	1.00000000	1.00000000	1.00000000	1.00000000
2	2.07750000	2.07800000	2.07850000	2.07900000	2.07950000
3	3.23850625	3.24008400	3.24166225	3.24324100	3.24482025
4	4.48949048	4.49281055	4.49613274	4.49945704	4.50278346
5	5.83742600	5.84324978	5.84907916	5.85491415	5.86075474
6	7.28982651	7.29902326	7.30823187	7.31745236	7.32668475
7	8.85478807	8.86834707	8.88192807	8.89553110	8.90915618
8	10.54103414	10.56007814	10.57915943	10.59827806	10.61743410
9	12.35796429	12.38376424	12.40962344	12.43554202	12.46152011
10	14.31570652	14.34969785	14.38377888	14.41794984	14.45221096
11	16.42517377	16.46897428	16.51290552	16.55696788	16.60116173
12	18.69812474	18.75355428	18.80916861	18.86496834	18.92095409
13	21.14722941	21.21633151	21.28568834	21.35530084	21.42516994
14	23.78613969	23.87120537	23.95661488	24.04236961	24.12847095
15	26.62956552	26.73315938	26.83720914	26.94171681	27.04668439
16	29.69335684	29.81834582	29.94393006	30.07011243	30.19689580
17	32.99459200	33.14417679	33.29452857	33.44565132	33.59754902
18	36.55167288	36.72942258	36.90814907	37.08785777	37.26855416
19	40.38442753	40.59431754	40.80543877	41.01779853	41.23140422
20	44.51422066	44.76067431	45.00866571	45.25820462	45.50930085
21	48.96407276	49.25200691	49.54184597	49.83360278	50.12729027
22	53.75878840	54.09366344	54.43088088	54.77045740	55.11240985
23	58.92509450	59.31296919	59.70370503	60.09732354	60.49384643
24	64.49178932	64.93938079	65.39044587	65.84501210	66.30310722
25	70.48990300	71.00465249	71.52359587	72.04676805	72.57420425
26	76.95287048	77.54301539	78.13819815	78.73846273	79.34385349
27	83.91671794	84.59137059	85.27204670	85.95880129	86.65168984
28	91.42026358	92.18949749	92.96590237	93.74954659	94.54049918
29	99.50533401	100.38027830	101.26372570	102.15576077	103.05646887
30	108.21699739	109.20994000	110.21292817	111.22606587	112.24945814
31	117.60381469	118.72831532	119.86464303	121.01292507	122.17329006
32	127.71811033	128.98912392	130.27401751	131.57294615	132.88606662
33	138.61626388	140.05027558	141.50052789	142.96720890	144.45050892
34	150.35902433	151.97419708	153.60831932	155.26161840	156.93432438
35	163.01184872	164.82818445	166.66657239	168.52728626	170.41060317
36	176.64526699	178.68478284	180.74989832	182.84094187	184.95824612
37	191.33527519	193.62219590	195.93876534	198.28537628	200.66242668
38	207.16375901	209.72472718	212.31995842	214.94992100	217.61508960
39	224.21895034	227.08325590	229.98707516	232.93096476	235.91548923
40	242.59591899	245.79574986	249.04106056	252.33251098	255.67077062

i	8.00	8.05	8.10	8.15	8.20
Years					
1	1.00000000	1.00000000	1.00000000	1.00000000	1.00000000
2	2.08000000	2.08050000	2.08100000	2.08150000	2.08200000
3	3.24640000	3.24798025	3.24956100	3.25114225	3.25272400
4	4.50611200	4.50944266	4.51277544	4.51611034	4.51944737
5	5.86660096	5.87245279	5.87831025	5.88417334	5.89004205
6	7.33592904	7.34518524	7.35445338	7.36373346	7.37302550
7	8.92280336	8.93647266	8.95016411	8.96387774	8.97761359
8	10.63662763	10.65585871	10.67512740	10.69443378	10.71377791
9	12.48755784	12.51365533	12.53981272	12.56603013	12.59230769
10	14.48656247	14.52100459	14.55553755	14.59016158	14.62487693
11	16.64548746	16.68994545	16.73453609	16.77925975	16.82411683
12	18.97712646	19.03348606	19.09003351	19.14676942	19.20369441
13	21.49529658	21.56568169	21.63632623	21.70723113	21.77839736
14	24.21492030	24.30171907	24.38886865	24.47637047	24.56422594
15	27.15211393	27.25800745	27.36436701	27.47119466	27.57849247
16	30.32428304	30.45227705	30.58088074	30.71009703	30.83992885
17	33.75022569	33.90368536	34.05793208	34.21296993	34.36880301
18	37.45024374	37.63293203	37.81662458	38.00132698	38.18704486
19	41.44626324	41.66238305	41.87977117	42.09843513	42.31838254
20	45.76196430	46.01620489	46.27203263	46.52945760	46.78848991
21	50.42292144	50.72050938	51.02006728	51.32160839	51.62514608
22	55.45675516	55.80351039	56.15269273	56.50431948	56.85840806
23	60.89329557	61.29569298	61.70106084	62.10942151	62.52079752
24	66.76475922	67.22999626	67.69884677	68.17133937	68.64750291
25	73.10593995	73.64201096	74.18245335	74.72730352	75.27659815
26	79.95441515	80.57019284	81.19123208	81.81757876	82.44927920
27	87.35076836	88.05609336	88.76772187	89.48571143	90.21012010
28	95.33882983	96.14460888	96.95790735	97.77879691	98.60734995
29	103.96593622	104.88424990	105.81149784	106.74776886	107.69315264
30	113.28321111	114.32743201	115.38222917	116.44771202	117.52399116
31	123.34586800	124.53079029	125.72818973	126.93820055	128.16095843
32	134.21353744	135.55551891	136.91217310	138.28366390	139.67015702
33	145.95062044	147.46773818	149.00205912	150.55378251	152.12310990
34	158.62667007	160.33889110	162.07122591	163.82391578	165.59720491
35	172.31680368	174.24617184	176.19899520	178.17556492	180.17617571
36	187.10214797	189.27298867	191.47111382	193.69687346	195.95062212
37	203.07031981	205.50946426	207.98027404	210.48316864	213.01857314
38	220.31594540	223.05297613	225.82667623	228.63754689	231.48609613
39	238.94122103	242.00874071	245.11863701	248.27150696	251.46795602
40	259.05651871	262.49044434	265.97324660	269.50563478	273.08832841

i	8.25	8.30	8.35	8.40	8.45
Years					
1	1.00000000	1.00000000	1.00000000	1.00000000	1.00000000
2	2.08250000	2.08300000	2.08350000	2.08400000	2.08450000
3	3.25430625	3.25588900	3.25747225	3.25905600	3.26064025
4	4.52278652	4.52612779	4.52947118	4.53281670	4.53616435
5	5.89591640	5.90179639	5.90768203	5.91357331	5.91947024
6	7.38232951	7.39164549	7.40097348	7.41031346	7.41966547
7	8.99137169	9.00515207	9.01895476	9.03277980	9.04662721
8	10.73315986	10.75257969	10.77203748	10.79153330	10.81106721
9	12.61864554	12.64504381	12.67150261	12.69802210	12.72460238
10	14.65968380	14.69458244	14.72957308	14.76465595	14.79983129
11	16.86910771	16.91423278	16.95949243	17.00488705	17.05041703
12	19.26080910	19.31811411	19.37561005	19.43329756	19.49117727
13	21.84982585	21.92151758	21.99347349	22.06569456	22.13818175
14	24.65243648	24.74100354	24.82992853	24.91921290	25.00885811
15	27.68626249	27.79450683	27.90322756	28.01242679	28.12210662
16	30.97037915	31.10145090	31.23314706	31.36547064	31.49842462
17	34.52543543	34.68287132	34.84111484	35.00017017	35.16004150
18	38.37378385	38.56154964	38.75034793	38.94018446	39.13106501
19	42.53962102	42.76215826	42.98600198	43.21115996	43.43764001
20	47.04913975	47.31141740	47.57533315	47.84089740	48.10812059
21	51.93069378	52.23826504	52.54787347	52.85953278	53.17325678
22	57.21497602	57.57404104	57.93562090	58.29973353	58.66639697
23	62.93521154	63.35268644	63.77324525	64.19691115	64.62370752
24	69.12736650	69.61095942	70.09831122	70.58945168	71.08441080
25	75.83037423	76.38866905	76.95152021	77.51896563	78.09104352
26	83.08638011	83.72892858	84.37697215	85.03055874	85.68973669
27	90.94100646	91.67842965	92.42244932	93.17312567	93.93051944
28	99.44363950	100.28773931	101.13972384	101.99966823	102.86764834
29	108.64773976	109.61162168	110.58489078	111.56764036	112.55996462
30	118.61117829	119.70938628	120.81872916	121.93932215	123.07128163
31	129.39660049	130.64526534	131.90709305	133.18222521	134.47080493
32	141.07182004	142.48882236	143.92133532	145.36953213	146.83358795
33	153.71024519	155.31539462	156.93876682	158.58057283	160.24102613
34	167.39134042	169.20657237	171.04315385	172.90134094	174.78139283
35	182.20112600	184.25071788	186.32525719	188.42505358	190.55042053
36	198.23271890	200.54352746	202.88341617	205.25275808	207.65193106
37	215.58691820	218.18864024	220.82418142	223.49398976	226.19851924
38	234.37283896	237.29829738	240.26300057	243.26748490	246.31229411
39	254.70859817	257.99405606	261.32496111	264.70195363	268.12568297
40	276.72205752	280.40756272	284.14559537	287.93691774	291.78230318

i	8.50	8.55	8.60	8.65	8.70
Years					
1	1.00000000	1.00000000	1.00000000	1.00000000	1.00000000
2	2.08500000	2.08550000	2.08600000	2.08650000	2.08700000
3	3.26222500	3.26381025	3.26539600	3.26698225	3.26856900
4	4.53951413	4.54286603	4.54622006	4.54957621	4.55293450
5	5.92537283	5.93128107	5.93719498	5.94311456	5.94903980
6	7.42902952	7.43840560	7.44779375	7.45719397	7.46660627
7	9.06049702	9.07438928	9.08830401	9.10224124	9.11620101
8	10.83063927	10.85024957	10.86989816	10.88958511	10.90931050
9	12.75124361	12.77794590	12.80470940	12.83153422	12.85842051
10	14.83509932	14.87046028	14.90591441	14.94146193	14.97710310
11	17.09608276	17.14188463	17.18782305	17.23389839	17.28011107
12	19.54924979	19.60751577	19.66597583	19.72463060	19.78348073
13	22.21093603	22.28395837	22.35724975	22.43081115	22.50464356
14	25.09886559	25.18923681	25.27997323	25.37107631	25.46254755
15	28.23226916	28.34291655	28.45405092	28.56567442	28.67778918
16	31.63201204	31.76623592	31.90109930	32.03660525	32.17275684
17	35.32073306	35.48224909	35.64459384	35.80777161	35.97178669
18	39.32299538	39.51598139	39.71002891	39.90514385	40.10133213
19	43.66544998	43.89459780	44.12509140	44.35693879	44.59014802
20	48.37701323	48.64758591	48.91984926	49.19381400	49.46949090
21	53.48905936	53.80695450	54.12695630	54.44907891	54.77333661
22	59.03562940	59.40744911	59.78187454	60.15892424	60.53861689
23	65.05365790	65.48678601	65.92311575	66.36267118	66.80547656
24	71.58321882	72.08590622	72.59250370	73.10304224	73.61755302
25	78.66779242	79.24925120	79.83545902	80.42645539	81.02228014
26	86.35455478	87.02506218	87.70130850	88.38334379	89.07121851
27	94.69469193	95.46570499	96.24362103	97.02850302	97.82041452
28	103.74374075	104.62802277	105.52057244	106.42146854	107.33079058
29	113.56195871	114.57371871	115.59534167	116.62692556	117.66856936
30	124.21472520	125.36977167	126.53654105	127.71515462	128.90573490
31	135.77297684	137.08888714	138.41868358	139.76251550	141.12053383
32	148.31367987	149.80998699	151.32269037	152.85197309	154.39802028
33	161.92034266	163.61874088	165.33644174	167.07366876	168.83064804
34	176.68357179	178.60814323	180.55537573	182.52554111	184.51891442
35	192.70167539	194.87913947	197.08313804	199.31400042	201.57205998
36	210.08131780	212.54130590	215.03228792	217.55466145	220.10882920
37	228.93822981	231.71358755	234.52506468	237.37313967	240.25829734
38	249.39797935	252.52509929	255.69422024	258.90591625	262.16076920
39	271.59680759	275.11599528	278.68392318	282.30127801	285.96875612
40	295.68253624	299.63841287	303.65074057	307.72033855	311.84803791

i	8.75	8.80	8.85	8.90	8.95
Years					
1	1.00000000	1.00000000	1.00000000	1.00000000	1.00000000
2	2.08750000	2.08800000	2.08850000	2.08900000	2.08950000
3	3.27015625	3.27174400	3.27333225	3.27492100	3.27651025
4	4.55629492	4.55965747	4.56302215	4.56638897	4.56975792
5	5.95497073	5.96090733	5.96684961	5.97279759	5.97875125
6	7.47603067	7.48546717	7.49491581	7.50437657	7.51384949
7	9.13018335	9.14418829	9.15821585	9.17226609	9.18633902
8	10.92907439	10.94887686	10.96871796	10.98859777	11.00851636
9	12.88536840	12.91237802	12.93944950	12.96658297	12.99377857
10	15.01283814	15.04866728	15.08459078	15.12060886	15.15672176
11	17.32646147	17.37295000	17.41957706	17.46634304	17.51324835
12	19.84252685	19.90176961	19.96120963	20.02084757	20.08068408
13	22.57874795	22.65312533	22.72777668	22.80270301	22.87790531
14	25.55438840	25.64660036	25.73918492	25.83214358	25.92547783
15	28.79039738	28.90350119	29.01710279	29.13120435	29.24580810
16	32.30955715	32.44700930	32.58511638	32.72388154	32.86330792
17	36.13664341	36.30234611	36.46889918	36.63630700	36.80457398
18	40.29859970	40.49695257	40.69639676	40.89693832	41.09858335
19	44.82472718	45.06068440	45.29802787	45.53676583	45.77690656
20	49.74689081	50.02602463	50.30690334	50.58953799	50.87393970
21	55.09974375	55.42831479	55.75906428	56.09200687	56.42715730
22	60.92097133	61.30600649	61.69374147	62.08419548	62.47738788
23	67.25155632	67.70093507	68.15363759	68.60968888	69.06911409
24	74.13606750	74.65861735	75.18523452	75.71595119	76.25079981
25	81.62297340	82.22857568	82.83912778	83.45467085	84.07524639
26	89.76498358	90.46469034	91.17039058	91.88213655	92.59998094
27	98.61941964	99.42558309	100.23897015	101.05964671	101.88767923
28	108.24861886	109.17503440	110.11011901	111.05395527	112.00662653
29	118.72037301	119.78243743	120.85486454	121.93775728	123.03121960
30	130.10840565	131.32329192	132.55052005	133.79021768	135.04251375
31	142.49289114	143.87974161	145.28124108	146.69754706	148.12881874
32	155.96101912	157.54115887	159.13863091	160.75362874	162.38634801
33	170.60760829	172.40478085	174.22239975	176.06070170	177.91992616
34	186.53577402	188.57640157	190.64108213	192.73010415	194.84375955
35	203.85765424	206.17112491	208.51281790	210.88308342	213.28227603
36	222.69519899	225.31418390	227.96620228	230.65167785	233.37103973
37	243.18102890	246.14183208	249.14121118	252.17967718	255.25774779
38	265.45936893	268.80231330	272.19020837	275.62366844	279.10331622
39	289.68706371	293.45691687	297.27904181	301.15417494	305.08306302
40	316.03468178	320.28112556	324.58823701	328.95689651	333.38799716

i	9.00	9.05	9.10	9.15	9.20
Years					
1	1.00000000	1.00000000	1.00000000	1.00000000	1.00000000
2	2.09000000	2.09050000	2.09100000	2.09150000	2.09200000
3	3.27810000	3.27969025	3.28128100	3.28287225	3.28446400
4	4.57312900	4.57650222	4.57987757	4.58325506	4.58663469
5	5.98471061	5.99067567	5.99664643	6.00262290	6.00860508
6	7.52333456	7.53283182	7.54234126	7.55186289	7.56139675
7	9.20043468	9.21455310	9.22869431	9.24285835	9.25704525
8	11.02847380	11.04847015	11.06850549	11.08857989	11.10869341
9	13.02103644	13.04835670	13.07573949	13.10318495	13.13069320
10	15.19292972	15.22923298	15.26563178	15.30212637	15.33871698
11	17.56029339	17.60747857	17.65480428	17.70227093	17.74987894
12	20.14071980	20.20095538	20.26139147	20.32202872	20.38286780
13	22.95338458	23.02914184	23.10517809	23.18149435	23.25809164
14	26.01918919	26.11327917	26.20774930	26.30260109	26.39783607
15	29.36091622	29.47653094	29.59265448	29.70928908	29.82643699
16	33.00339868	33.14415699	33.28558604	33.42768904	33.57046919
17	36.97370456	37.14370320	37.31457437	37.48632258	37.65895236
18	41.30133797	41.50520834	41.71020064	41.91632110	42.12357598
19	46.01845839	46.26142969	46.50582890	46.75166448	46.99894497
20	51.16011964	51.44808908	51.73785932	52.02944178	52.32284790
21	56.76453041	57.10414114	57.44600452	57.79013570	58.13654991
22	62.87333815	63.27206591	63.67359093	64.07793312	64.48511250
23	69.53193858	69.99818788	70.46788771	70.94106400	71.41774285
24	76.78981305	77.33302388	77.88046549	78.43217135	78.98817519
25	84.70089623	85.33166254	85.96758785	86.60871503	87.25508731
26	93.32397689	94.05417800	94.79063835	95.53341246	96.28255535
27	102.72313481	103.56608111	104.41658644	105.27471970	106.14055044
28	112.96821694	113.93881145	114.91849580	115.90735655	116.90548108
29	124.13535646	125.25027389	126.37607892	127.51287968	128.66078534
30	136.30753855	137.58542367	138.87630210	140.18030817	141.49757759
31	149.57521702	151.03690451	152.51404559	154.00680636	155.51535473
32	164.03698655	165.70574437	167.39282374	169.09842915	170.82276736
33	179.80031534	181.70211424	183.62557070	185.57093541	187.53846196
34	196.98234372	199.14615558	201.33549763	203.55067600	205.79200046
35	215.71075465	218.16888266	220.65702792	223.17556286	225.72486450
36	236.12472257	238.91316654	241.73681746	244.59612686	247.49155203
37	258.37594760	261.53480811	264.73486785	267.97667247	271.26077482
38	282.62978288	286.20370824	289.82574082	293.49653800	297.21676610
39	309.06646334	313.10514384	317.19988324	321.35147122	325.56070859
40	337.88244504	342.44115936	347.06507261	351.75513084	356.51229378

i	9.25	9.30	9.35	9.40	9.45
Years					
1	1.00000000	1.00000000	1.00000000	1.00000000	1.00000000
2	2.09250000	2.09300000	2.09350000	2.09400000	2.09450000
3	3.28605625	3.28764900	3.28924225	3.29083600	3.29243025
4	4.59001645	4.59340036	4.59678640	4.60017458	4.60356491
5	6.01459298	6.02058659	6.02658593	6.03259099	6.03860179
6	7.57094283	7.58050114	7.59007171	7.59965455	7.60924966
7	9.27125504	9.28548775	9.29974342	9.31402208	9.32832375
8	11.12884613	11.14903811	11.16926943	11.18954015	11.20985035
9	13.15826439	13.18589865	13.21359612	13.24135693	13.26918121
10	15.37540385	15.41218723	15.44906736	15.48604448	15.52311883
11	17.79762871	17.84552064	17.89355515	17.94173266	17.99005356
12	20.44390936	20.50515406	20.56660256	20.62825553	20.69011362
13	23.33497098	23.41213339	23.48957990	23.56731155	23.64532936
14	26.49345579	26.58946179	26.68585562	26.78263883	26.87981299
15	29.94410045	30.06228174	30.18098312	30.30020688	30.41995531
16	33.71392975	33.85807394	34.00290504	34.14842633	34.29464109
17	37.83246825	38.00687482	38.18217667	38.35837840	38.53548467
18	42.33197156	42.54151418	42.75221018	42.96406597	43.17708797
19	47.24767893	47.49787500	47.74954184	48.00268818	48.25732279
20	52.61808923	52.91517737	53.21412400	53.51494086	53.81763979
21	58.48526249	58.83628887	59.18964459	59.54534530	59.90340675
22	64.89514927	65.30806373	65.72387636	66.14260776	66.56427869
23	71.89795057	72.38171366	72.86905880	73.36001289	73.85460302
24	79.54851100	80.11321303	80.68231580	81.25585411	81.83386301
25	87.90674827	88.56374184	89.22611233	89.89390439	90.56716307
26	97.03812248	97.80016983	98.56875383	99.34393140	100.12575997
27	107.01414881	107.89558562	108.78493231	109.68226096	110.58764429
28	117.91295758	118.92987509	119.95632348	120.99239349	122.03817668
29	129.81990615	130.99035347	132.17223973	133.36567847	134.57078437
30	142.82824747	144.17245634	145.53034414	146.90205225	148.28772350
31	157.03986036	158.58049478	160.13743132	161.71084516	163.30091337
32	172.56604745	174.32848080	176.11028115	177.91166461	179.73284968
33	189.52840684	191.54102951	193.57659244	195.63536108	197.71760398
34	208.05978447	210.35434526	212.67600383	215.02508502	217.40191755
35	228.30531453	230.91729937	233.56121019	236.23744301	238.94639876
36	250.42355613	253.39260821	256.39918334	259.44376266	262.52683344
37	274.58773507	277.95812077	281.37250698	284.83147635	288.33561920
38	300.98710056	304.80822600	308.68083638	312.60563512	316.58333522
39	329.82840737	334.15539102	338.54249459	342.99056482	347.50046040
40	361.33753505	366.23184239	371.19621783	376.23167792	381.33925390

i	9.50	9.55	9.60	9.65	9.70
Years					
1	1.00000000	1.00000000	1.00000000	1.00000000	1.00000000
2	2.09500000	2.09550000	2.09600000	2.09650000	2.09700000
3	3.29402500	3.29562025	3.29721600	3.29881225	3.30040900
4	4.60695738	4.61035198	4.61374874	4.61714763	4.62054867
5	6.04461833	6.05064060	6.05666861	6.06270238	6.06874189
6	7.61885707	7.62847678	7.63810880	7.64775316	7.65740986
7	9.34264849	9.35699631	9.37136725	9.38576134	9.40017861
8	11.23020009	11.25058945	11.27101850	11.29148731	11.31199594
9	13.29706910	13.32502075	13.35303628	13.38111583	13.40925955
10	15.56029067	15.59756023	15.63492776	15.67239351	15.70995772
11	18.03851828	18.08712723	18.13588083	18.18477948	18.23382362
12	20.75217752	20.81444788	20.87692539	20.93961070	21.00250451
13	23.72363438	23.80222765	23.88111022	23.96028314	24.03974745
14	26.97737965	27.07534040	27.17369680	27.27245046	27.37160295
15	30.54023072	30.66103540	30.78237170	30.90424193	31.02664844
16	34.44155263	34.58916428	34.73747938	34.88650127	35.03623334
17	38.71350013	38.89242947	39.07227740	39.25304865	39.43474797
18	43.39128265	43.60665649	43.82321603	44.04096784	44.25991852
19	48.51345450	48.77109218	49.03024477	49.29092124	49.55313062
20	54.12223267	54.42873149	54.73714827	55.04749514	55.35978429
21	60.26384478	60.62667534	60.99191450	61.35957842	61.72968337
22	66.98891003	67.41652284	67.84713829	68.28077774	68.71746265
23	74.35285649	74.85480077	75.36046357	75.86987279	76.38305653
24	82.41637785	83.00343424	83.59506807	84.19131551	84.79221302
25	91.24593375	91.93026221	92.62019461	93.31577746	94.01705768
26	100.91429745	101.70960225	102.51173329	103.32074999	104.13671227
27	111.50115571	112.42286927	113.35285969	114.29120236	115.23797336
28	123.09376551	124.15925328	125.23473422	126.32030339	127.41605678
29	135.78767323	137.01646197	138.25726870	139.51021266	140.77541429
30	149.68750218	151.10153409	152.52996650	153.97294818	155.43062947
31	164.90781489	166.53173060	168.17284328	169.83133768	171.50740053
32	181.57405731	183.43551087	185.31743623	187.22006177	189.14361838
33	199.82359275	201.95360216	204.10791011	206.28679773	208.49054937
34	219.80683406	222.24017116	224.70226948	227.19347371	229.71413266
35	241.68848330	244.46410751	247.27368735	250.11764393	252.99640352
36	265.64888921	268.81042978	272.01196134	275.25399657	278.53705467
37	291.88553369	295.48182582	299.12510963	302.81600723	306.55514897
38	320.61465939	324.70034019	328.84112015	333.03775193	337.29099842
39	352.07305203	356.70922268	361.40986769	366.17589499	371.00822526
40	386.51999197	391.77495344	397.10521499	402.51186886	407.99602311

i	9.75	9.80	9.85	9.90	9.95
Years					
1	1.00000000	1.00000000	1.00000000	1.00000000	1.00000000
2	2.09750000	2.09800000	2.09850000	2.09900000	2.09950000
3	3.30200625	3.30360400	3.30520225	3.30680100	3.30840025
4	4.62395186	4.62735719	4.63076467	4.63417430	4.63758607
5	6.07478717	6.08083820	6.08689499	6.09295755	6.09902589
6	7.66707891	7.67676034	7.68645415	7.69616035	7.70587897
7	9.41461911	9.42908285	9.44356988	9.45808023	9.47261392
8	11.33254447	11.35313297	11.37376152	11.39443017	11.41513901
9	13.43746756	13.46574000	13.49407702	13.52247876	13.55094534
10	15.74762064	15.78538252	15.82324361	15.86120415	15.89926440
11	18.28301366	18.33235001	18.38183311	18.43146336	18.48124121
12	21.06560749	21.12892031	21.19244367	21.25617824	21.32012471
13	24.11950422	24.19955450	24.27989937	24.36053988	24.44147712
14	27.47115588	27.57111085	27.67146946	27.77223333	27.87340409
15	31.14959358	31.27307971	31.39710920	31.52168443	31.64680780
16	35.18667895	35.33784152	35.48972446	35.64233119	35.79566517
17	39.61738015	39.80094999	39.98546231	40.17092198	40.35733386
18	44.48007472	44.70144309	44.92403035	45.14784325	45.37288858
19	49.81688200	50.08218451	50.34904734	50.61747974	50.88749099
20	55.67402799	55.99023859	56.30842851	56.62861023	56.95079634
21	62.10224572	62.47728197	62.85480871	63.23484264	63.61740058
22	69.15721468	69.60005561	70.04600737	70.49509207	70.94733194
23	76.90004311	77.42086106	77.94553910	78.47410618	79.00659146
24	85.39779732	86.00810544	86.62317470	87.24304269	87.86774731
25	94.72408256	95.43689977	96.15555741	96.88010392	97.61058817
26	104.95968061	105.78971595	106.62687981	107.47123421	108.32284170
27	116.19324946	117.15710812	118.12962747	119.11088639	120.10096444
28	128.52209129	129.63850471	130.76539578	131.90286414	133.05101041
29	142.05299519	143.34307817	144.64578726	145.96124769	147.28958594
30	156.90316222	158.39069983	159.89339731	161.41141122	162.94489974
31	173.20122053	174.91298842	176.64289694	178.39114093	180.15791727
32	191.08833954	193.05446128	195.04222229	197.05186388	199.08363004
33	210.71945264	212.97379849	215.25388119	217.55999840	219.89245122
34	232.26459927	234.84523074	237.45638848	240.09843824	242.77175012
35	255.91039770	258.86006335	261.84584275	264.86818363	267.92753926
36	281.86166148	285.22834956	288.63765826	292.09013381	295.58632941
37	310.34317347	314.18072782	318.06846760	322.00705706	325.99716919
38	341.60163289	345.97043914	350.39821166	354.88575571	359.43388752
39	375.90779209	380.87554218	385.91243551	391.01944552	396.19755933
40	413.55880182	419.20134531	424.92481040	430.73037063	436.61921649

i	10.00	10.05	10.10	10.15	10.20
Years					
1	1.00000000	1.00000000	1.00000000	1.00000000	1.00000000
2	2.10000000	2.10050000	2.10100000	2.10150000	2.10200000
3	3.31000000	3.31160025	3.31320100	3.31480225	3.31640400
4	4.64100000	4.64441608	4.64783430	4.65125468	4.65467721
5	6.10510000	6.11117989	6.11726557	6.12335703	6.12945428
6	7.71561000	7.72535347	7.73510939	7.74487777	7.75465862
7	9.48717100	9.50175149	9.51635544	9.53098286	9.54563380
8	11.43588810	11.45667752	11.47750733	11.49837762	11.51928845
9	13.57947691	13.60807361	13.63673558	13.66546295	13.69425587
10	15.93742460	15.97568501	16.01404587	16.05250744	16.09106997
11	18.53116706	18.58124135	18.63146450	18.68183694	18.73235910
12	21.38428377	21.44865611	21.51324242	21.57804339	21.64305973
13	24.52271214	24.60424604	24.68607990	24.76821480	24.85065182
14	27.97498336	28.07697277	28.17937397	28.28218860	28.38541831
15	31.77248169	31.89870854	32.02549074	32.15283074	32.28073098
16	35.94972986	36.10452874	36.26006531	36.41634306	36.57336554
17	40.54470285	40.73303388	40.92233190	41.11260188	41.30384882
18	45.59917313	45.82670379	46.05548742	46.28553097	46.51684140
19	51.15909045	51.43228752	51.70709165	51.98351237	52.26155923
20	57.27499949	57.60123241	57.92950791	58.25983887	58.59223827
21	64.00249944	64.39015627	64.78038821	65.17321252	65.56864657
22	71.40274939	71.86136698	72.32320742	72.78829359	73.25664852
23	79.54302433	80.08343436	80.62785137	81.17630539	81.72882667
24	88.49732676	89.13181951	89.77126436	90.41570039	91.06516699
25	98.34705943	99.08956737	99.83816206	100.59289397	101.35381402
26	109.18176538	110.04806889	110.92181642	111.80307271	112.69190305
27	121.09994191	122.10789981	123.12491988	124.15108459	125.18647717
28	134.20993611	135.37974375	136.56053679	137.75241968	138.95549784
29	148.63092972	149.98540799	151.35315101	152.73429028	154.12895862
30	164.49402269	166.05894150	167.63981926	169.23682074	170.85011240
31	181.94342496	183.74786512	185.57144100	187.41435804	189.27682386
32	201.13776745	203.21452556	205.31415654	207.43691539	209.58305989
33	222.25154420	224.63758538	227.05088635	229.49176230	231.96053200
34	245.47669862	248.21366271	250.98302588	253.78517617	256.62050627
35	271.02436848	274.15913581	277.33231149	280.54437155	283.79579791
36	299.12680533	302.71212896	306.34287495	310.01962527	313.74296929
37	330.03948586	334.13469792	338.28350532	342.48661723	346.74475216
38	364.04343445	368.71523506	373.45013936	378.24900888	383.11271688
39	401.44777789	406.77111619	412.16860343	417.64128328	423.19021400
40	442.59255568	448.65161336	454.79763238	461.03187353	467.35561583

i	10.25	10.30	10.35	10.40	10.45
Years					
1	1.00000000	1.00000000	1.00000000	1.00000000	1.00000000
2	2.10250000	2.10300000	2.10350000	2.10400000	2.10450000
3	3.31800625	3.31960900	3.32121225	3.32281600	3.32442025
4	4.65810189	4.66152873	4.66495772	4.66838886	4.67182217
5	6.13555733	6.14166619	6.14778084	6.15390131	6.16002758
6	7.76445196	7.77425780	7.78407616	7.79390704	7.80375046
7	9.56030829	9.57500636	9.58972804	9.60447337	9.61924239
8	11.54023989	11.56123201	11.58226489	11.60333860	11.62445322
9	13.72311448	13.75203891	13.78102931	13.81008582	13.83920858
10	16.12973371	16.16849892	16.20736584	16.24633475	16.28540588
11	18.78303141	18.83385430	18.88482821	18.93595356	18.98723079
12	21.70829213	21.77374130	21.83940793	21.90529273	21.97139641
13	24.93339208	25.01643665	25.09978665	25.18344317	25.26740733
14	28.48906477	28.59312963	28.69761457	28.80252126	28.90785140
15	32.40919390	32.53822198	32.66781767	32.79798347	32.92872187
16	36.73113628	36.88965884	37.04893680	37.20897375	37.36977330
17	41.49607775	41.68929370	41.88350176	42.07870703	42.27491461
18	46.74942572	46.98329095	47.21844420	47.45489256	47.69264319
19	52.54124185	52.82256992	53.10555317	53.39020138	53.67652441
20	58.92671914	59.26329462	59.60197792	59.94278233	60.28572121
21	65.96670785	66.36741397	66.77078264	67.17683169	67.58557907
22	73.72829541	74.20325761	74.68155864	75.16322218	75.64827209
23	82.28544569	82.84619314	83.41109996	83.98019729	84.55351652
24	91.71970387	92.37935104	93.04414881	93.71413781	94.38935899
25	102.12097352	102.89442419	103.67421821	104.46040814	105.25304701
26	113.58837331	114.49254989	115.40449979	116.32429059	117.25199042
27	126.23118157	127.28528252	128.34886552	129.42201681	130.50482342
28	140.16987768	141.39566662	142.63297310	143.88190656	145.14257747
29	155.53729014	156.95942029	158.39548582	159.84562484	161.30997681
30	172.47986238	174.12624058	175.78941860	177.46956982	179.16686939
31	191.15904828	193.06124336	194.98362342	196.92640508	198.88980724
32	211.75285072	213.94655142	216.16442845	218.40675121	220.67379210
33	234.45751792	236.98304622	239.53744679	242.12105334	244.73420337
34	259.48941351	262.39229998	265.32957254	268.30164288	271.30892763
35	287.08707840	290.41870688	293.79118329	297.20501374	300.66071056
36	317.51350393	321.33183369	325.19857076	329.11433517	333.07975482
37	351.05863808	355.42901255	359.85662284	364.34222603	368.88658919
38	388.04214849	393.03820085	398.10178330	403.23381754	408.43523777
39	428.81646871	434.52113554	440.30531787	446.17013456	452.11672011
40	473.77015675	480.27681250	486.87691827	493.57182856	500.36291736

i	10.50	10.55	10.60	10.65	10.70
Years					
1	1.00000000	1.00000000	1.00000000	1.00000000	1.00000000
2	2.10500000	2.10550000	2.10600000	2.10650000	2.10700000
3	3.32602500	3.32763025	3.32923600	3.33084225	3.33244900
4	4.67525763	4.67869524	4.68213502	4.68557695	4.68902104
5	6.16615968	6.17229759	6.17844133	6.18459089	6.19074629
6	7.81360644	7.82347499	7.83335611	7.84324983	7.85315615
7	9.63403512	9.64885160	9.66369186	9.67855593	9.69344386
8	11.64560881	11.66680544	11.68804319	11.70932214	11.73064235
9	13.86839773	13.89765341	13.92697577	13.95636495	13.98582108
10	16.32457949	16.36385585	16.40323520	16.44271781	16.48230394
11	19.03866034	19.09024264	19.14197813	19.19386726	19.24591046
12	22.03771967	22.10426324	22.17102782	22.23801412	22.30522288
13	25.35168024	25.43626301	25.52115677	25.60636263	25.69188172
14	29.01360666	29.11978876	29.22639938	29.33344025	29.44091307
15	33.06003536	33.19192647	33.32439772	33.45745163	33.59109077
16	37.53133908	37.69367471	37.85678387	38.02067023	38.18533748
17	42.47212968	42.67035740	42.86960297	43.06987161	43.27116859
18	47.93170330	48.17208010	48.41378088	48.65681294	48.90118363
19	53.96453214	54.25423455	54.54564165	54.83876352	55.13361027
20	60.63080802	60.97805630	61.32747967	61.67909183	62.03290657
21	67.99704286	68.41124124	68.82819251	69.24791511	69.67042758
22	76.13673236	76.62862719	77.12398092	77.62281807	78.12516333
23	85.13108926	85.71294736	86.29912290	86.88964819	87.48455580
24	95.06985363	95.75566330	96.44682992	97.14339573	97.84540328
25	106.05218826	106.85788578	107.67019390	108.48916737	109.31486143
26	118.18766803	119.13139273	120.08323445	121.04326370	122.01155160
27	131.59737317	132.69975467	133.81205730	134.93437128	136.06678762
28	146.41509736	147.69957878	148.99613537	150.30488182	151.62593389
29	162.78868258	164.28188434	165.78972572	167.31235174	168.84990882
30	180.88149425	182.61362314	184.36343665	186.13111720	187.91684906
31	200.87405114	202.87936038	204.90596094	206.95408118	209.02395191
32	222.96582651	225.28313290	227.62599279	229.99469082	232.38951477
33	247.37723830	250.05050343	252.75434803	255.48912539	258.25519285
34	274.35184832	277.43083154	280.54630892	283.69871725	286.88849849
35	304.15879239	307.69978427	311.28421767	314.91263064	318.58556782
36	337.09546560	341.16211150	345.28034474	349.45082580	353.67422358
37	373.49048948	378.15471427	382.88006128	387.66733875	392.51736550
38	413.70699088	419.05003662	424.46534778	429.95391032	435.51672361
39	458.14622492	464.25981549	470.45867464	476.74400177	483.11701304
40	507.25157854	514.23922602	521.32729416	528.51723796	535.81053343

i	10.75	10.80	10.85	10.90	10.95
Years					
1	1.00000000	1.00000000	1.00000000	1.00000000	1.00000000
2	2.10750000	2.10800000	2.10850000	2.10900000	2.10950000
3	3.33405625	3.33566400	3.33727225	3.33888100	3.34049025
4	4.69246730	4.69591571	4.69936629	4.70281903	4.70627393
5	6.19690753	6.20307461	6.20924753	6.21542630	6.22161093
6	7.86307509	7.87300667	7.88295089	7.89290777	7.90287732
7	9.70835566	9.72329139	9.73825106	9.75323472	9.76824239
8	11.75200390	11.77340686	11.79485130	11.81633730	11.83786493
9	14.01534432	14.04493480	14.07459267	14.10431807	14.13411114
10	16.52199383	16.56178775	16.60168597	16.64168874	16.68179631
11	19.29810817	19.35046083	19.40296890	19.45563281	19.50845301
12	22.37265479	22.44031060	22.50819102	22.57629678	22.64462861
13	25.77771518	25.86386415	25.95032975	26.03711313	26.12421545
14	29.54881957	29.65716148	29.76594053	29.87515847	29.98481704
15	33.72531767	33.86013491	33.99554507	34.13155074	34.26815451
16	38.35078932	38.51702949	38.68406172	38.85188977	39.02051742
17	43.47349917	43.67686867	43.88128241	44.08674575	44.29326408
18	49.14690033	49.39397049	49.64240155	49.89220104	50.14337650
19	55.43019212	55.72851930	56.02860212	56.33045096	56.63407623
20	62.38893777	62.74719938	63.10770545	63.47047011	63.83550757
21	70.09574858	70.52389692	70.95489149	71.38875135	71.82549565
22	78.63104155	79.14047778	79.65349722	80.17012525	80.69038743
23	88.08387852	88.68764938	89.29590167	89.90866890	90.52598485
24	98.55289546	99.26591552	99.98450700	100.70871381	101.43858019
25	110.14733173	110.98663439	111.83282601	112.68596362	113.54610472
26	122.98816989	123.97319091	124.96668763	125.96873365	126.97940319
27	137.20939815	138.36229553	139.52557324	140.69932562	141.88364784
28	152.95940845	154.30542344	155.66409794	157.03555211	158.41990727
29	170.40254486	171.97040917	173.55365256	175.15242729	176.76688712
30	189.72081843	191.54321337	193.38422387	195.24404187	197.12286126
31	211.11580641	213.22988041	215.36641215	217.52564243	219.70781457
32	234.81075560	237.25870749	239.73366787	242.23593745	244.76582026
33	261.05291183	263.88264790	266.74477084	269.63965464	272.56767758
34	290.11609985	293.38197388	296.68657847	300.03037699	303.41383828
35	322.30358058	326.06722705	329.87707224	333.73368808	337.63765357
36	357.95121550	362.28248758	366.66873458	371.11066008	375.60897664
37	397.43097116	402.40899623	407.45229228	412.56172203	417.73815958
38	441.15480056	446.86916783	452.66086599	458.53094973	464.48048805
39	489.57894162	496.13103795	502.77456995	509.51082326	516.34110149
40	543.20867785	550.71319005	558.32561079	566.04750299	573.88045211

i	11.00	11.05	11.10	11.15	11.20
Years					
1	1.00000000	1.00000000	1.00000000	1.00000000	1.00000000
2	2.11000000	2.11050000	2.11100000	2.11150000	2.11200000
3	3.34210000	3.34371025	3.34532100	3.34693225	3.34854400
4	4.70973100	4.71319023	4.71665163	4.72011520	4.72358093
5	6.22780141	6.23399775	6.24019996	6.24640804	6.25262199
6	7.91285957	7.92285451	7.93286216	7.94288254	7.95291566
7	9.78327412	9.79832993	9.81340986	9.82851394	9.84364221
8	11.85943427	11.88104538	11.90269835	11.92439324	11.94613014
9	14.16397204	14.19390090	14.22389787	14.25396309	14.28409671
10	16.72200896	16.76232695	16.80275053	16.84327998	16.88391554
11	19.56142995	19.61456408	19.66785584	19.72130569	19.77491408
12	22.71318724	22.78197341	22.85098784	22.92023128	22.98970446
13	26.21163784	26.29938147	26.38744749	26.47583706	26.56455136
14	30.09491800	30.20546312	30.31645416	30.42789290	30.53978111
15	34.40535898	34.54316680	34.68158057	34.82060296	34.96023660
16	39.18994847	39.36018673	39.53123602	39.70310018	39.87578310
17	44.50084281	44.70948736	44.91920321	45.12999586	45.34187080
18	50.39593551	50.64988571	50.90523477	51.16199039	51.42016033
19	56.93948842	57.24669809	57.55571583	57.86655232	58.17921829
20	64.20283215	64.57245822	64.94440029	65.31867291	65.69529074
21	72.26514368	72.70771486	73.15322872	73.60170493	74.05316330
22	81.21430949	81.74191735	82.27323711	82.80829503	83.34711759
23	91.14788353	91.77439922	92.40556643	93.04141993	93.68199476
24	102.17415072	102.91547033	103.66258430	104.41553825	105.17437817
25	114.41330730	115.28762980	116.16913116	117.05787077	117.95390853
26	127.99877110	129.02691290	130.06390472	131.10982336	132.16474629
27	143.07863592	144.28438677	145.50099814	146.72856866	147.96719787
28	159.81728587	161.22781151	162.65160893	164.08880407	165.53952403
29	178.39718732	180.04348468	181.70593752	183.38470572	185.07995072
30	199.02087793	200.93828974	202.87529659	204.83210041	206.80890520
31	221.91317450	224.14197075	226.39445451	228.67087961	230.97150259
32	247.32362369	249.90965852	252.52423896	255.16768268	257.84031088
33	275.52922230	278.52467579	281.55442949	284.61887930	287.71842569
34	306.83743675	310.30165246	313.80697116	317.35388435	320.94288937
35	341.58955480	345.58998506	349.63954496	353.73884245	357.88849298
36	380.16440582	384.77767841	389.44953445	394.18072338	398.97200419
37	422.98249046	428.29561187	433.67843277	439.13187404	444.65686866
38	470.51056441	476.62227699	482.81673881	489.09507800	495.45843795
39	523.26672650	530.28903859	537.40939682	544.62917919	551.94978301
40	581.82606641	589.88597736	598.06183986	606.35533267	614.76815870

i	11.25	11.30	11.35	11.40	11.45
Years					
1	1.00000000	1.00000000	1.00000000	1.00000000	1.00000000
2	2.11250000	2.11300000	2.11350000	2.11400000	2.11450000
3	3.35015625	3.35176900	3.35338225	3.35499600	3.35661025
4	4.72704883	4.73051890	4.73399114	4.73746554	4.74094212
5	6.25884182	6.26506753	6.27129913	6.27753662	6.28378000
6	7.96296153	7.97302016	7.98309158	7.99317579	8.00327281
7	9.85879470	9.87397144	9.88917247	9.90439783	9.91964754
8	11.96790910	11.98973021	12.01159355	12.03349918	12.05544719
9	14.31429888	14.34456973	14.37490942	14.40531809	14.43579589
10	16.92465750	16.96550611	17.00646164	17.04752435	17.08869452
11	19.82868147	19.88260830	19.93669503	19.99094213	20.04535004
12	23.05940813	23.12934304	23.19950992	23.26990953	23.34054262
13	26.65359155	26.74295880	26.83265430	26.92267922	27.01303475
14	30.65212060	30.76491314	30.87816056	30.99186465	31.10602723
15	35.10048416	35.24134833	35.38283178	35.52493722	35.66766735
16	40.04928863	40.22362069	40.39878319	40.57478006	40.75161526
17	45.55483360	45.76888983	45.98404508	46.20030499	46.41767521
18	51.67975238	51.94077438	52.20323420	52.46713976	52.73249902
19	58.49372453	58.81008188	59.12830128	59.44839369	59.77037015
20	66.07426854	66.45562114	66.83936347	67.22551057	67.61407754
21	74.50762375	74.96510633	75.42563123	75.88921877	76.35588941
22	83.88973142	84.43616334	84.98644037	85.54058971	86.09863875
23	94.32732620	94.97744980	95.63240136	96.29221694	96.95693289
24	105.93915040	106.70990163	107.48667891	108.26952967	109.05850171
25	118.85730482	119.76812051	120.68641697	121.61225606	122.54570015
26	133.22875161	134.30191813	135.38432529	136.47605325	137.57718282
27	149.21698617	150.47803487	151.75044621	153.03432332	154.32977025
28	167.00389711	168.48205282	169.97412186	171.48023617	173.00052895
29	186.79183554	188.52052478	190.26618469	192.02898310	193.80908951
30	208.80591704	210.82334408	212.86139665	214.92028717	217.00023026
31	233.29658270	235.64638197	238.02116517	240.42119991	242.84675662
32	260.54244826	263.27442313	266.03656742	268.82921670	271.65271026
33	290.85347368	294.02443294	297.23171782	300.47574740	303.75694558
34	324.57448947	328.24919386	331.96751779	335.72998261	339.53711585
35	362.08911954	366.34135277	370.64583106	375.00320062	379.41411561
36	403.82414549	408.73792563	413.71413288	418.75356549	423.85703185
37	450.25436185	455.92531123	461.67068697	467.49147196	473.38866200
38	501.90797756	508.44487140	515.07030994	521.78549976	528.59166380
39	559.37262504	566.89914187	574.53079011	582.26904674	590.11540930
40	623.30204536	631.95874490	640.74003479	649.64771807	658.68362367

i	11.50	11.55	11.60	11.65	11.70
Years					
1	1.00000000	1.00000000	1.00000000	1.00000000	1.00000000
2	2.11500000	2.11550000	2.11600000	2.11650000	2.11700000
3	3.35822500	3.35984025	3.36145600	3.36307225	3.36468900
4	4.74442088	4.74790180	4.75138490	4.75487017	4.75835761
5	6.29002928	6.29628446	6.30254554	6.30881254	6.31508545
6	8.01338264	8.02350531	8.03364083	8.04378920	8.05395045
7	9.93492165	9.95022017	9.96554316	9.98089064	9.99626265
8	12.07743764	12.09947061	12.12154617	12.14366440	12.16582539
9	14.46634296	14.49695946	14.52764553	14.55840131	14.58922696
10	17.12997240	17.17135828	17.21285241	17.25445506	17.29616651
11	20.09991923	20.15465016	20.20954329	20.26459908	20.31981799
12	23.41140994	23.48251225	23.55385031	23.62542487	23.69723670
13	27.10372209	27.19474242	27.28609694	27.37778686	27.46981339
14	31.22065013	31.33573517	31.45128419	31.56729903	31.68378156
15	35.81102489	35.95501258	36.09963315	36.24488937	36.39078400
16	40.92929275	41.10781653	41.28719060	41.46741898	41.64850573
17	46.63616142	46.85576934	47.07650471	47.29837329	47.52138090
18	52.99931998	53.26761070	53.53737926	53.80863378	54.08138246
19	60.09424178	60.42001973	60.74771525	61.07733962	61.40890421
20	68.00507958	68.39853201	68.79445022	69.19284969	69.59374600
21	76.82566374	77.29856246	77.77460644	78.25381667	78.73621428
22	86.66061507	87.22654643	87.79646079	88.37038632	88.94835135
23	97.62658580	98.30121254	98.98085024	99.66553632	100.35530846
24	109.85364317	110.65500259	111.46262887	112.27657130	113.09687955
25	123.48681213	124.43565538	125.39229382	126.35679186	127.32921446
26	138.68779553	139.80797358	140.93779990	142.07735811	143.22673255
27	155.63689201	156.95579453	158.28658469	159.62937033	160.98426026
28	174.53513459	176.08418880	177.64782851	179.22619198	180.81941871
29	195.60667507	197.42191260	199.25497662	201.10604334	202.97529070
30	219.10144270	221.22414351	223.36855391	225.53489739	227.72339971
31	245.29810861	247.77553209	250.27930616	252.80971294	255.36703748
32	274.50739111	277.39360604	280.31170568	283.26204449	286.24498086
33	307.07574108	310.43256754	313.82786354	317.26207268	320.73564362
34	343.38945131	347.28752909	351.23189571	355.22310414	359.26171392
35	383.87923821	388.39923870	392.97479561	397.60659578	402.29533445
36	429.02535060	434.25935077	439.55987190	444.92776418	450.36388858
37	479.36326592	485.41630578	491.54881704	497.76184871	504.05646355
38	535.49004150	542.48188910	549.56847982	556.75110408	564.03106978
39	598.07139627	606.13854729	614.31842348	622.61260771	631.02270495
40	667.84960685	677.14754951	686.57936060	696.14697651	705.85236143

i	11.75	11.80	11.85	11.90	11.95
Years					
1	1.00000000	1.00000000	1.00000000	1.00000000	1.00000000
2	2.11750000	2.11800000	2.11850000	2.11900000	2.11950000
3	3.36630625	3.36792400	3.36954225	3.37116100	3.37278025
4	4.76184723	4.76533903	4.76883301	4.77232916	4.77582749
5	6.32136428	6.32764904	6.33393972	6.34023633	6.34653887
6	8.06412459	8.07431162	8.08451157	8.09472445	8.10495027
7	10.01165923	10.02708040	10.04252620	10.05799666	10.07349183
8	12.18802919	12.21027588	12.23256555	12.25489826	12.27727410
9	14.62012262	14.65108844	14.68212457	14.71323116	14.74440836
10	17.33798702	17.37991687	17.42195633	17.46410567	17.50636515
11	20.37520050	20.43074706	20.48645815	20.54233424	20.59837579
12	23.76928656	23.84157522	23.91410345	23.98687201	24.05988170
13	27.56217773	27.65488109	27.74792470	27.84130978	27.93503756
14	31.80073361	31.91815706	32.03605378	32.15442565	32.27327455
15	36.53731981	36.68449959	36.83232615	36.98080230	37.12993086
16	41.83045489	42.01327055	42.19695680	42.38151777	42.56695760
17	47.74553334	47.97083647	48.19729618	48.42491839	48.65370903
18	54.35563350	54.63139517	54.90867578	55.18748368	55.46782726
19	61.74242044	62.07789981	62.41535386	62.75479424	63.09623261
20	69.99715484	70.40309198	70.81157330	71.22261475	71.63623241
21	79.22182053	79.71065684	80.20274473	80.69810591	81.19676218
22	89.53038445	90.11651434	90.70676998	91.30118051	91.89977527
23	101.05020462	101.75026304	102.45552223	103.16602099	103.88179841
24	113.92360366	114.75679407	115.59650161	116.44277749	117.29567332
25	128.30962709	129.29809577	130.29468705	131.29946801	132.31250628
26	144.38600828	145.55527108	146.73460746	147.92410470	149.12385078
27	162.35136425	163.73079306	165.12265845	166.52707316	167.94415095
28	182.42764955	184.05102664	185.68969348	187.34379487	189.01347699
29	204.86289837	206.76904779	208.69392215	210.63770645	212.60058749
30	229.93428893	232.16779543	234.42415193	236.70359352	239.00635770
31	257.95156788	260.56359529	263.20341393	265.87132115	268.56761744
32	289.26087710	292.31009953	295.39301848	298.51000837	301.66144772
33	324.24903016	327.80269128	331.39709117	335.03269937	338.70999073
34	363.34829121	367.48340885	371.66764648	375.90159059	380.18583462
35	407.04171542	411.84645109	416.71026258	421.63387987	426.61804186
36	455.86911699	461.44433232	467.09042870	472.80831157	478.59889786
37	510.43373823	516.89476353	523.44064450	530.07250065	536.79146615
38	571.40970247	578.88834563	586.46836087	594.15112823	601.93804636
39	639.55034251	648.19717041	656.96486164	665.85511249	674.86964290
40	715.69750776	725.68443652	735.81519774	746.09187088	756.51656522

i	12.00	12.05	12.10	12.15	12.20
Years					
1	1.00000000	1.00000000	1.00000000	1.00000000	1.00000000
2	2.12000000	2.12050000	2.12100000	2.12150000	2.12200000
3	3.37440000	3.37602025	3.37764100	3.37926225	3.38088400
4	4.77932800	4.78283069	4.78633556	4.78984261	4.79335185
5	6.35284736	6.35916179	6.36548216	6.37180849	6.37814077
6	8.11518904	8.12544078	8.13570551	8.14598322	8.15627395
7	10.08901173	10.10455640	10.12012587	10.13572018	10.15133937
8	12.29969314	12.32215544	12.34466110	12.36721019	12.38980277
9	14.77565631	14.80697518	14.83836510	14.86982622	14.90135871
10	17.54873507	17.59121568	17.63380727	17.67651011	17.71932447
11	20.65458328	20.71095717	20.76749795	20.82420609	20.88108206
12	24.13313327	24.20662751	24.28036520	24.35434713	24.42857407
13	28.02910926	28.12352613	28.21828939	28.31340030	28.40886011
14	32.39260238	32.51241103	32.63270241	32.75347844	32.87474104
15	37.27971466	37.43015656	37.58125940	37.73302607	37.88545945
16	42.75328042	42.94049042	43.12859179	43.31758874	43.50748550
17	48.88367407	49.11481952	49.34715140	49.58067577	49.81539873
18	55.74971496	56.03315527	56.31815672	56.60472788	56.89287738
19	63.43968075	63.78515048	64.13265368	64.48220232	64.83380842
20	72.05244244	72.47126111	72.89270477	73.31678990	73.74353304
21	81.69873554	82.20404807	82.71272205	83.22477987	83.74024407
22	92.50258380	93.10963587	93.72096142	94.33659062	94.95655385
23	104.60289386	105.32934699	106.06119775	106.79848638	107.54125342
24	118.15524112	119.02153330	119.89460268	120.77450248	121.66128634
25	133.33387006	134.36362806	135.40184960	136.44860453	137.50396327
26	150.33393446	151.55444525	152.78547341	154.02710998	155.27944679
27	169.37400660	170.81675590	172.27251569	173.74140384	175.22353930
28	190.69888739	192.40017498	194.11749009	195.85098441	197.60081109
29	214.58275388	216.58439607	218.60570639	220.64687902	222.70811005
30	241.33268434	243.68281580	246.05699686	248.45547482	250.87849947
31	271.29260646	274.04659510	276.82989348	279.64281501	282.48567641
32	304.84771924	308.06920981	311.32631059	314.61941703	317.94892893
33	342.42944555	346.19154959	349.99679417	353.84567620	357.73869826
34	384.52097901	388.90763132	393.34640627	397.83792586	402.38281944
35	431.66349649	436.77100089	441.94132143	447.17523385	452.47352342
36	484.46311607	490.40190650	496.41622132	502.50702477	508.67529327
37	543.59869000	550.49533623	557.48258410	564.56162827	571.73367905
38	609.83053280	617.83002425	625.93797677	634.15586611	642.48518790
39	684.01019674	693.27854217	702.67647196	712.20580384	721.86838082
40	767.09142034	777.81860650	788.70032507	799.73880901	810.93632328

i	12.25	12.30	12.35	12.40	12.45
Years					
1	1.00000000	1.00000000	1.00000000	1.00000000	1.00000000
2	2.12250000	2.12300000	2.12350000	2.12400000	2.12450000
3	3.38250625	3.38412900	3.38575225	3.38737600	3.38900025
4	4.79686327	4.80037687	4.80389265	4.80741062	4.81093078
5	6.38447902	6.39082322	6.39717340	6.40352954	6.40989166
6	8.16657770	8.17689448	8.18722431	8.19756720	8.20792318
7	10.16698346	10.18265250	10.19834651	10.21406554	10.22980961
8	12.41243894	12.43511876	12.45784231	12.48060966	12.50342091
9	14.93296271	14.96463836	14.99638583	15.02820526	15.06009681
10	17.76225064	17.80528888	17.84843948	17.89170272	17.93507886
11	20.93812634	20.99533941	21.05272176	21.11027385	21.16799618
12	24.50304682	24.57776616	24.65273289	24.72794781	24.80341171
13	28.50467005	28.60083140	28.69734541	28.79421334	28.89143646
14	32.99649214	33.11873366	33.24146756	33.36469579	33.48842030
15	38.03856242	38.19233790	38.34678881	38.50191807	38.65772863
16	43.69828632	43.88999546	44.08261723	44.27615591	44.47061585
17	50.05132639	50.28846491	50.52682045	50.76639924	51.00720752
18	57.18261388	57.47394609	57.76688278	58.06143275	58.35760485
19	65.18748408	65.54324146	65.90109280	66.26105041	66.62312666
20	74.17295087	74.60506016	75.03987776	75.47742066	75.91770593
21	84.25913736	84.78148256	85.30730267	85.83662083	86.36946032
22	95.58088168	96.20960491	96.84275455	97.48036181	98.12245813
23	108.28953969	109.04338632	109.80283474	110.56792667	111.33870416
24	122.55500830	123.45572283	124.36348482	125.27834958	126.20037283
25	138.56799682	139.64077674	140.72237520	141.81286493	142.91231925
26	156.54257643	157.81659228	159.10158854	160.39766018	161.70490299
27	176.71904204	178.22803313	179.75063472	181.28697004	182.83716342
28	199.36712469	201.15008121	202.94983811	204.76655432	206.60039026
29	224.78959746	226.89154120	229.01414312	231.15760706	233.32213885
30	253.32632315	255.79920076	258.29738979	260.82115034	263.37074514
31	285.35879774	288.26250246	291.19711743	294.16297298	297.16040291
32	321.31525046	324.71879026	328.15996143	331.63918163	335.15687307
33	361.67636864	365.65920146	369.68771667	373.76244015	377.88390377
34	406.98172380	411.63528324	416.34414968	421.10898273	425.93044978
35	457.83698497	463.26642308	468.76265217	474.32649659	479.95879078
36	514.92201563	521.24819312	527.65483971	534.14298216	540.71366023
37	578.99996254	586.36172088	593.82021241	601.37671195	609.03251093
38	650.92745795	659.48421254	668.15700865	676.94742423	685.85705855
39	731.66607155	741.60077069	751.67439921	761.88890484	772.24626233
40	822.29516532	833.81766548	845.50618752	857.36312904	869.39092199

i	12.50	12.55	12.60	12.65	12.70
Years					
1	1.00000000	1.00000000	1.00000000	1.00000000	1.00000000
2	2.12500000	2.12550000	2.12600000	2.12650000	2.12700000
3	3.39062500	3.39225025	3.39387600	3.39550225	3.39712900
4	4.81445313	4.81797766	4.82150438	4.82503328	4.82856438
5	6.41625977	6.42263385	6.42901393	6.43540000	6.44179206
6	8.21829224	8.22867440	8.23906968	8.24947809	8.25989965
7	10.24557877	10.26137304	10.27719246	10.29303707	10.30890691
8	12.52627611	12.54917535	12.57211871	12.59510626	12.61813808
9	15.09206063	15.12409686	15.15620567	15.18838721	15.22064162
10	17.97856820	18.02217102	18.06588758	18.10971819	18.15366311
11	21.22588923	21.28395348	21.34218942	21.40059754	21.45917832
12	24.87912538	24.95508964	25.03130529	25.10777313	25.18449397
13	28.98901606	29.08695339	29.18524975	29.28390643	29.38292470
14	33.61264306	33.73736604	33.86259122	33.98832059	34.11455614
15	38.81422345	38.97140548	39.12927772	39.28784314	39.44710477
16	44.66600138	44.86231687	45.05956671	45.25775530	45.45688707
17	51.24925155	51.49253764	51.73707211	51.98286135	52.22991173
18	58.65540799	58.95485111	59.25594320	59.55869331	59.86311052
19	66.98733399	67.35368492	67.72219204	68.09286801	68.46572556
20	76.36075074	76.80657238	77.25518824	77.70661582	78.16087271
21	86.90584458	87.44579721	87.98934196	88.53650272	89.08730354
22	98.76907515	99.42024477	100.07599905	100.73637031	101.40139109
23	112.11520955	112.89748548	113.68557493	114.47952115	115.27936776
24	127.12961074	128.06611991	129.00995737	129.96118058	130.91984746
25	144.02081209	145.13841796	146.26521200	147.40126992	148.54666809
26	163.02341360	164.35328941	165.69462871	167.04753057	168.41209494
27	184.40134030	185.97962724	187.57215192	189.17904318	190.80043099
28	208.45150783	210.32007045	212.20624307	214.11019215	216.03208573
29	235.50794631	237.71523930	239.94422969	242.19513145	244.46816062
30	265.94643960	268.54850183	271.17720263	273.83281558	276.51561702
31	300.18974455	303.25133881	306.34553017	309.47266675	312.63310038
32	338.71346262	342.30938183	345.94506697	349.62095910	353.33750412
33	382.05264545	386.26920925	390.53414540	394.84801043	399.21136715
34	430.80922613	435.74599501	440.74144772	445.79628374	450.91121078
35	485.66037939	491.43211738	497.27487014	503.18951364	509.17693454
36	547.36792682	554.10684811	560.93150378	567.84298711	574.84240523
37	616.78891767	624.64725755	632.60887325	640.67512498	648.84739070
38	694.88753238	704.04048837	713.31759128	722.72052829	732.25100931
39	782.74847393	793.39756966	804.19560778	815.14467512	826.24688750
40	881.59203317	893.96896465	906.52425436	919.26047653	932.18024221

i	12.75	12.80	12.85	12.90	12.95
Years					
1	1.00000000	1.00000000	1.00000000	1.00000000	1.00000000
2	2.12750000	2.12800000	2.12850000	2.12900000	2.12950000
3	3.39875625	3.40038400	3.40201225	3.40364100	3.40527025
4	4.83209767	4.83563315	4.83917082	4.84271069	4.84625275
5	6.44819013	6.45459420	6.46100428	6.46742037	6.47384248
6	8.27033437	8.28078225	8.29124332	8.30171760	8.31220508
7	10.32480200	10.34072238	10.35666809	10.37263917	10.38863564
8	12.64121425	12.66433485	12.68749994	12.71070962	12.73396395
9	15.25296907	15.28536971	15.31784368	15.35039116	15.38301228
10	18.19772263	18.24189703	18.28618660	18.33059162	18.37511237
11	21.51793226	21.57685985	21.63596157	21.69523794	21.75468943
12	25.26146862	25.33869791	25.41618264	25.49392363	25.57192171
13	29.48230587	29.58205124	29.68216211	29.78263978	29.88348557
14	34.24129987	34.36855380	34.49631994	34.62460031	34.75339695
15	39.60706561	39.76772869	39.92909705	40.09117375	40.25396185
16	45.65696647	45.85799796	46.05998602	46.26293516	46.46684991
17	52.47822970	52.72782170	52.97869422	53.23085380	53.48430698
18	60.16920398	60.47698287	60.78645643	61.09763394	61.41052473
19	68.84077749	69.21803668	69.59751608	69.97922872	70.36318769
20	78.61797662	79.07794538	79.54079690	80.00654922	80.47522049
21	89.64176864	90.19992238	90.76178930	91.32739407	91.89676154
22	102.07109414	102.74551245	103.42467922	104.10862791	104.79739216
23	116.08515864	116.89693804	117.71475051	118.53864091	119.36865445
24	131.88601637	132.85974611	133.84109595	134.83012558	135.82689520
25	149.70148346	150.86579361	152.03967677	153.22321178	154.41647813
26	169.78842260	171.17661520	172.57677524	173.98900610	175.41341205
27	192.43644648	194.08722194	195.75289086	197.43358789	199.12944891
28	217.97209341	219.93038635	221.90713733	223.90252073	225.91671254
29	246.76353531	249.08147580	251.42220448	253.78594590	256.17292681
30	279.22588607	281.96390471	284.72995776	287.52433293	290.34732084
31	315.82718654	319.05528451	322.31775733	325.61497187	328.94729889
32	357.09515282	360.89436093	364.73558914	368.61930324	372.54597409
33	403.62478481	408.08883912	412.60411235	417.17119336	421.79067774
34	456.08694487	461.32421053	466.62374079	471.98627731	477.41257050
35	515.23803034	521.37370948	527.58489148	533.87250708	540.23749838
36	581.93087921	589.10954429	596.37955003	603.74206049	611.19825442
37	657.12706631	665.51556596	674.01432221	682.62478630	691.34842837
38	741.91076727	751.70155841	761.62516262	771.68338373	781.87804985
39	837.50439009	848.91935788	860.49399601	872.23054023	884.13125730
40	945.28619983	958.58103569	972.06747450	985.74827992	999.62625512

i	13.00	13.05	13.10	13.15	13.20
Years					
1	1.00000000	1.00000000	1.00000000	1.00000000	1.00000000
2	2.13000000	2.13050000	2.13100000	2.13150000	2.13200000
3	3.40690000	3.40853025	3.41016100	3.41179225	3.41342400
4	4.84979700	4.85334345	4.85689209	4.86044293	4.86399597
5	6.48027061	6.48670477	6.49314495	6.49959118	6.50604344
6	8.32270579	8.33321974	8.34374694	8.35428742	8.36484117
7	10.40465754	10.42070492	10.43677779	10.45287621	10.46900020
8	12.75726302	12.78060691	12.80399568	12.82742943	12.85090823
9	15.41570722	15.44847611	15.48131912	15.51423640	15.54722812
10	18.41974915	18.46450224	18.50937192	18.55435849	18.59946223
11	21.81431654	21.87411978	21.93409965	21.99425663	22.05459124
12	25.65017769	25.72869241	25.80746670	25.88650138	25.96579729
13	29.98470079	30.08628678	30.18824484	30.29057631	30.39328253
14	34.88271190	35.01254720	35.14290491	35.27378710	35.40519582
15	40.41746444	40.58168461	40.74662545	40.91229010	41.07868167
16	46.67173482	46.87759445	47.08443339	47.29225625	47.50106765
17	53.73906035	53.99512053	54.25249416	54.51118794	54.77120858
18	61.72513819	62.04148375	62.35957090	62.67940916	63.00100811
19	70.74940616	71.13789738	71.52867469	71.92175146	72.31714118
20	80.94682896	81.42139299	81.89893107	82.37946178	82.86300382
21	92.46991672	93.04688478	93.62769104	94.21236100	94.80092033
22	105.49100590	106.18950324	106.89291857	107.60128647	108.31464181
23	120.20483667	121.04723342	121.89589090	122.75085564	123.61217453
24	136.83146543	137.84389738	138.86425261	139.89259316	140.92898157
25	155.61955594	156.83252598	158.05546970	159.28846916	160.53160713
26	176.85009821	178.29917062	179.76073623	181.23490286	182.72177927
27	200.84061098	202.56721239	204.30939267	206.06729258	207.84105414
28	227.94989040	230.00223361	232.07392311	234.16514156	236.27607328
29	258.58337616	261.01752509	263.47560704	265.95785767	268.46451496
30	293.19921506	296.08031212	298.99091156	301.93131596	304.90183093
31	332.31511301	335.71879285	339.15872098	342.63528401	346.14887261
32	376.51607771	380.53009532	384.58851343	388.69182385	392.84052380
33	426.46316781	431.18927276	435.96960869	440.80479869	445.69547294
34	482.90337962	488.45947285	494.08162742	499.77062972	505.52727537
35	546.68081897	553.20343406	559.80632062	566.49046753	573.25687572
36	618.74932544	626.39648220	634.14094862	641.98396400	649.92678331
37	700.18673775	709.14122313	718.21341289	727.40485527	736.71711871
38	792.21101365	802.68415275	813.29936997	824.05859374	834.96377838
39	896.19844543	908.43443468	920.84158744	933.42229882	946.17899712
40	1013.70424333	1027.98512841	1042.47183539	1057.16733111	1072.07462474

i	13.25	13.30	13.35	13.40	13.45
Years					
1	1.00000000	1.00000000	1.00000000	1.00000000	1.00000000
2	2.13250000	2.13300000	2.13350000	2.13400000	2.13450000
3	3.41505625	3.41668900	3.41832225	3.41995600	3.42159025
4	4.86755120	4.87110864	4.87466827	4.87823010	4.88179414
5	6.51250174	6.51896609	6.52543648	6.53191294	6.53839545
6	8.37540822	8.38598858	8.39658226	8.40718927	8.41780964
7	10.48514981	10.50132506	10.51752599	10.53375263	10.55000503
8	12.87443216	12.89800129	12.92161571	12.94527549	12.96898071
9	15.58029442	15.61343546	15.64665140	15.67994240	15.71330862
10	18.64468343	18.69002238	18.73547936	18.78105468	18.82674863
11	22.11510398	22.17579535	22.23666586	22.29771601	22.35894632
12	26.04535526	26.12517613	26.20526075	26.28560996	26.36622460
13	30.49636483	30.59982456	30.70366306	30.80788169	30.91248180
14	35.53713317	35.66960123	35.80260208	35.93613784	36.07021061
15	41.24580332	41.41365819	41.58224946	41.75158031	41.92165393
16	47.71087225	47.92167473	48.13347976	48.34629207	48.56011639
17	55.03256283	55.29525747	55.55929931	55.82469521	56.09145204
18	63.32437740	63.64952671	63.97646577	64.30520437	64.63575234
19	72.71485741	73.11491376	73.51732395	73.92210175	74.32926103
20	83.34957602	83.83919729	84.33188669	84.82766338	85.32654664
21	95.39339484	95.98981053	96.59019357	97.19457028	97.80296716
22	109.03301965	109.75645533	110.48498441	111.21864270	111.95746625
23	124.47989476	125.35406389	126.23472983	127.12194082	128.01574546
24	141.97348081	143.02615439	144.08706626	145.15628089	146.23386322
25	161.78496702	163.04863292	164.32268960	165.60722252	166.90231783
26	184.22147515	185.73410110	187.25976867	188.79859034	190.35067957
27	209.63082061	211.43673655	213.25894778	215.09760145	216.95284598
28	238.40690434	240.55782251	242.72901731	244.92068004	247.13300376
29	270.99581916	273.55201290	276.13334112	278.74005117	281.37239277
30	307.90276520	310.93443062	313.99714216	317.09121803	320.21697959
31	349.69988159	353.28870989	356.91576064	360.58144124	364.28616335
32	397.03511590	401.27610830	405.56401469	409.89935437	414.28265232
33	450.64226876	455.64583071	460.70681065	465.82586785	471.00366906
34	511.35236937	517.24672619	523.21116987	529.24653415	535.35366254
35	580.10655831	587.04054078	594.05986105	601.16556972	608.35873016
36	657.97067729	666.11693270	674.36685250	682.72175606	691.18297936
37	746.15179203	755.71048475	765.39482731	775.20647138	785.14709009
38	846.01690447	857.21997922	868.57503676	880.08413854	891.74937370
39	959.11414432	972.23023645	985.52980416	999.01541310	1012.68966447
40	1087.19676844	1102.53685790	1118.09803302	1133.88347846	1149.89642434

i	13.50	13.55	13.60	13.65	13.70
Years					
1	1.00000000	1.00000000	1.00000000	1.00000000	1.00000000
2	2.13500000	2.13550000	2.13600000	2.13650000	2.13700000
3	3.42322500	3.42486025	3.42649600	3.42813225	3.42976900
4	4.88536038	4.88892881	4.89249946	4.89607230	4.89964735
5	6.54488403	6.55137867	6.55787938	6.56438617	6.57089904
6	8.42844337	8.43909048	8.44975098	8.46042488	8.47111221
7	10.56628322	10.58258724	10.59891711	10.61527288	10.63165458
8	12.99273146	13.01652781	13.04036984	13.06425763	13.08819126
9	15.74675021	15.78026733	15.81386014	15.84752879	15.88127346
10	18.87256148	18.91849355	18.96454511	19.01071648	19.05700793
11	22.42035728	22.48194942	22.54372325	22.60567927	22.66781801
12	26.44710552	26.52825357	26.60966961	26.69135450	26.77330908
13	31.01746476	31.12283193	31.22858468	31.33472438	31.44125242
14	36.20482251	36.33997566	36.47567220	36.61191426	36.74870401
15	42.09247354	42.26404236	42.43636361	42.60944056	42.78327645
16	48.77495747	48.99082010	49.20770907	49.42562920	49.64458533
17	56.35957673	56.62907622	56.89995750	57.17222758	57.44589352
18	64.96811959	65.30231605	65.63835172	65.97623665	66.31598093
19	74.73881573	75.15077987	75.56516755	75.98199295	76.40127032
20	85.82855586	86.33371055	86.84203034	87.35353498	87.86824435
21	98.41541090	99.03192833	99.65254647	100.27729251	100.90619383
22	112.70149137	113.45075461	114.20529279	114.96514294	115.73034238
23	128.91619271	129.82333187	130.73721260	131.65788495	132.58539929
24	147.31987872	148.41439333	149.51747352	150.62918624	151.74959899
25	168.20806235	169.52454363	170.85184992	172.19007017	173.53929405
26	191.91615077	193.49511929	195.08770151	196.69401474	198.31417734
27	218.82483112	220.71370796	222.61962891	224.54274776	226.48321963
28	249.36618332	251.62041538	253.89589844	256.19283283	258.51142072
29	284.03061807	286.71498167	289.42574063	292.16315451	294.92748536
30	323.37475151	326.56486168	329.78764136	333.04342510	336.33255085
31	368.03034296	371.81440044	375.63876058	379.50385262	383.41011032
32	418.71443926	423.19525170	427.72563202	432.30612850	436.93729544
33	476.24088856	481.53820831	486.89631797	492.31591504	497.79770491
34	541.53340851	547.78663553	554.11421722	560.51703745	566.99599048
35	615.64041866	623.01172465	630.47375076	638.02761306	645.67444118
36	699.75187518	708.42981334	717.21818086	726.11838224	735.13183962
37	795.21837833	805.42205305	815.75985346	826.23354142	836.84490165
38	903.57285941	915.55674123	927.70319353	940.01441982	952.49265318
39	1026.55519543	1040.61467967	1054.87082785	1069.32638813	1083.98414666
40	1166.14014681	1182.61796876	1199.33326044	1216.28944011	1233.48997475

i	13.75	13.80	13.85	13.90	13.95
Years					
1	1.00000000	1.00000000	1.00000000	1.00000000	1.00000000
2	2.13750000	2.13800000	2.13850000	2.13900000	2.13950000
3	3.43140625	3.43304400	3.43468225	3.43632100	3.43796025
4	4.90322461	4.90680407	4.91038574	4.91396962	4.91755570
5	6.57741799	6.58394303	6.59047417	6.59701140	6.60355473
6	8.48181297	8.49252717	8.50325484	8.51399598	8.52475061
7	10.64806225	10.66449592	10.68095563	10.69744142	10.71395332
8	13.11217081	13.13619636	13.16026799	13.18438578	13.20854981
9	15.91509430	15.94899146	15.98296511	16.01701540	16.05114251
10	19.10341976	19.14995228	19.19660577	19.24338054	19.29027689
11	22.73013998	22.79264569	22.85533567	22.91821044	22.98127051
12	26.85553423	26.93803080	27.02079966	27.10384169	27.18715775
13	31.54817018	31.65547905	31.76318042	31.87127568	31.97976625
14	36.88604358	37.02393516	37.16238090	37.30138300	37.44094365
15	42.95787457	43.13323821	43.30937066	43.48627524	43.66395528
16	49.86458233	50.08562508	50.30771850	50.53086750	50.75507705
17	57.72096240	57.99744134	58.27533751	58.55465808	58.83541030
18	66.65759473	67.00108825	67.34647175	67.69375556	68.04295003
19	76.82301400	77.24723843	77.67395809	78.10318758	78.53494156
20	88.38617843	88.90735733	89.43180129	89.95953065	90.49056591
21	101.53927796	102.17657264	102.81810576	103.46390541	104.11399985
22	116.50092868	117.27693967	118.05841341	118.84538827	119.63790283
23	133.51980638	134.46115734	135.40950367	136.36489724	137.32739028
24	152.87877975	154.01679705	155.16371993	156.31961795	157.48456122
25	174.89961197	176.27111505	177.65389514	179.04804485	180.45365751
26	199.94830862	201.59652892	203.25895962	204.93572308	206.62694273
27	228.44120105	230.41684991	232.41032552	234.42178859	236.45140125
28	260.85186620	263.21437520	265.59915561	268.00641720	270.43637172
29	297.71899780	300.53795898	303.38463866	306.25930919	309.16224557
30	339.65535999	343.01219732	346.40341111	349.82935317	353.29037883
31	387.35797199	391.34788055	395.38028355	399.45563326	403.57438668
32	441.61969314	446.35388807	451.14045282	455.97996628	460.87301362
33	503.34240095	508.95072462	514.62340554	520.36118160	526.16479902
34	573.55198108	580.18592462	586.89874721	593.69138584	600.56478848
35	653.41537848	661.25158221	669.18422370	677.21448847	685.34357648
36	744.25999302	753.50430056	762.86623868	772.34730237	781.94900540
37	847.59574206	858.48789404	869.52321273	880.70357740	892.03089165
38	965.14015659	977.95922341	990.95217770	1004.12137466	1017.46920104
39	1098.84692813	1113.91759624	1129.19905431	1144.69424573	1160.40615458
40	1250.93838074	1268.63822452	1286.59312333	1304.80674589	1323.28281314

i	14.00	14.05	14.10	14.15	14.20
Years					
1	1.00000000	1.00000000	1.00000000	1.00000000	1.00000000
2	2.14000000	2.14050000	2.14100000	2.14150000	2.14200000
3	3.43960000	3.44124025	3.44288100	3.44452225	3.44616400
4	4.92114400	4.92473451	4.92832722	4.93192215	4.93551929
5	6.61010416	6.61665970	6.62322136	6.62978913	6.63636303
6	8.53551874	8.54630039	8.55709557	8.56790429	8.57872658
7	10.73049137	10.74705560	10.76364605	10.78026275	10.79690575
8	13.23276016	13.25701691	13.28132014	13.30566993	13.33006637
9	16.08534658	16.11962778	16.15398628	16.18842223	16.22293579
10	19.33729510	19.38443549	19.43169834	19.47908397	19.52659267
11	23.04451641	23.10794867	23.17156781	23.23537435	23.29936883
12	27.27074871	27.35461546	27.43875887	27.52317983	27.60787921
13	32.08865353	32.19793893	32.30762387	32.41770977	32.52819806
14	37.58106503	37.72174935	37.86299884	38.00481570	38.14720218
15	43.84241413	44.02165514	44.20168167	44.38249713	44.56410489
16	50.98035211	51.20669768	51.43411879	51.66262047	51.89220778
17	59.11760141	59.40123871	59.68632954	59.97288126	60.26090129
18	68.39406560	68.74711275	69.10210200	69.45904396	69.81794927
19	78.96923479	79.40608209	79.84549839	80.28749868	80.73209807
20	91.02492766	91.56263662	92.10371366	92.64817975	93.19605599
21	104.76841753	105.42718707	106.09033729	106.75789718	107.42989594
22	120.43599598	121.23970685	122.04907484	122.86413963	123.68494117
23	138.29703542	139.27388566	140.25799440	141.24941539	142.24820281
24	158.65862038	159.84186660	161.03437161	162.23620767	163.44744761
25	181.87082723	183.29964886	184.74021800	186.19263106	187.65698517
26	208.33274304	210.05324952	211.78858874	213.53888835	215.30427707
27	238.49932707	240.56573108	242.65077975	244.75464105	246.87748441
28	272.88923286	275.36521629	277.86453970	280.38742276	282.93408720
29	312.09372546	315.05402918	318.04343980	321.06224308	324.11072758
30	356.78684702	360.31912028	363.88756481	367.49255048	371.13445090
31	407.73700561	411.94395668	416.19571145	420.49274637	424.83554292
32	465.82018639	470.82208260	475.87930676	480.99246998	486.16219002
33	532.03501249	537.97258520	543.97828901	550.05290448	556.19722100
34	607.51991423	614.55773343	621.67922777	628.88539047	636.17722639
35	693.57270223	701.90309497	710.33599888	718.87267322	727.51439253
36	791.67288054	801.52047982	811.49337472	821.59315648	831.82143627
37	903.50708382	915.13410723	926.91394056	938.84858812	950.94008022
38	1030.99807555	1044.71044929	1058.60880618	1072.69566334	1086.97357161
39	1176.33780613	1192.49226742	1208.87264785	1225.48209970	1242.32381878
40	1342.02509898	1361.03743099	1380.32369119	1399.88781681	1419.73380105

i	14.25	14.30	14.35	14.40	14.45
Years					
1	1.00000000	1.00000000	1.00000000	1.00000000	1.00000000
2	2.14250000	2.14300000	2.14350000	2.14400000	2.14450000
3	3.44780625	3.44944900	3.45109225	3.45273600	3.45438025
4	4.93911864	4.94272021	4.94632399	4.94992998	4.95353820
5	6.64294305	6.64952920	6.65612148	6.66271990	6.66932447
6	8.58956243	8.60041187	8.61127491	8.62215157	8.63304185
7	10.81357508	10.83027077	10.84699286	10.86374139	10.88051640
8	13.35450953	13.37899949	13.40353634	13.42812015	13.45275102
9	16.25752713	16.29219642	16.32694380	16.36176946	16.39667354
10	19.57422475	19.62198050	19.66986024	19.71786426	19.76599287
11	23.36355178	23.42792372	23.49248518	23.55723671	23.62217884
12	27.69285791	27.77811681	27.86365681	27.94947880	28.03558368
13	32.63909016	32.75038751	32.86209156	32.97420374	33.08672552
14	38.29016050	38.43369292	38.57780170	38.72248908	38.86775736
15	44.74650838	44.92971101	45.11371624	45.29852751	45.48414829
16	52.12288582	52.35465969	52.58753452	52.82151547	53.05660772
17	60.55039705	60.84137602	61.13384572	61.42781370	61.72328754
18	70.17882863	70.54169279	70.90655259	71.27341887	71.64230259
19	81.17931171	81.62915486	82.08164288	82.53679119	82.99461531
20	93.74736363	94.30212401	94.86035864	95.42208912	95.98733722
21	108.10636294	108.78732774	109.47282010	110.16286996	110.85750745
22	124.51151966	125.34391561	126.18216978	127.02632323	127.87641728
23	143.25441121	144.26809554	145.28931115	146.31811378	147.35455958
24	164.66816481	165.89843321	167.13832730	168.38792216	169.64729344
25	189.13337830	190.62190915	192.12267727	193.63578295	195.16132734
26	217.08488470	218.88084216	220.69228145	222.51933570	224.36213914
27	249.01948078	251.18080259	253.36162384	255.56212004	257.78246824
28	285.50475679	288.09965736	290.71901686	293.36306532	296.03203490
29	327.18918463	330.29790837	333.43719578	336.60734673	339.80866395
30	374.81364344	378.53050926	382.28543338	386.07880466	389.91101589
31	429.22458763	433.66037209	438.14339307	442.67415253	447.25315768
32	491.38909136	496.67380530	502.01696997	507.41923049	512.88123897
33	562.41203688	568.69815945	575.05640516	581.48759968	587.99257800
34	643.55575214	651.02199625	658.57699930	666.22181403	673.95750552
35	736.26244682	745.11814172	754.08279870	763.15775525	772.34436507
36	842.17984549	852.67003598	863.29368032	874.05247201	884.94812582
37	963.19047347	975.60185113	988.17632344	1000.91602798	1013.82313000
38	1101.44511594	1116.11291584	1130.97962586	1146.04793601	1161.32057228
39	1259.40104496	1276.71706281	1294.27520217	1312.07883880	1330.13139498
40	1439.86569387	1460.28760279	1481.00369368	1502.01819158	1523.33538155

i	14.50	14.55	14.60	14.65	14.70
Years					
1	1.00000000	1.00000000	1.00000000	1.00000000	1.00000000
2	2.14500000	2.14550000	2.14600000	2.14650000	2.14700000
3	3.45602500	3.45767025	3.45931600	3.46096225	3.46260900
4	4.95714863	4.96076127	4.96437614	4.96799322	4.97161252
5	6.67593518	6.68255204	6.68917505	6.69580423	6.70243956
6	8.64394578	8.65486336	8.66579461	8.67673955	8.68769818
7	10.89731791	10.91414598	10.93100062	10.94788189	10.96478981
8	13.47742901	13.50215422	13.52692671	13.55174659	13.57661391
9	16.43165622	16.46671765	16.50185801	16.53707746	16.57237616
10	19.81424637	19.86262507	19.91112928	19.95975931	20.00851546
11	23.68731209	23.75263702	23.81815416	23.88386405	23.94976723
12	28.12197235	28.20864571	28.29560467	28.38285013	28.47038301
13	33.19965834	33.31300366	33.42676295	33.54093767	33.65552931
14	39.01360880	39.16004569	39.30707034	39.45468504	39.60289212
15	45.67058207	45.85783234	46.04590261	46.23479640	46.42451726
16	53.29281647	53.53014694	53.76860439	54.00819407	54.24892130
17	62.02027486	62.31878332	62.61882063	62.92039451	63.22351273
18	72.01321471	72.38616630	72.76116844	73.13823230	73.51736910
19	83.45513085	83.91835349	84.38429903	84.85298333	85.32442236
20	96.55612482	97.12847393	97.70440669	98.28394539	98.86711245
21	111.55676292	112.26066688	112.96925007	113.68254339	114.40057798
22	128.73249354	129.59459391	130.46276058	131.33703600	132.21746294
23	148.39870511	149.45060733	150.51032362	151.57791177	152.65342999
24	170.91651735	172.19567069	173.48483087	174.78407585	176.09348420
25	196.69941236	198.25014078	199.81361618	201.38994296	202.97922638
26	226.22082715	228.09553626	229.98640414	231.89356960	233.81717266
27	260.02284709	262.28343679	264.56441914	266.86597755	269.18829704
28	298.72615992	301.44567684	304.19082434	306.96184326	309.75897671
29	343.04145311	346.30602283	349.60268469	352.93175330	356.29354628
30	393.78246381	397.69354915	401.64467666	405.63625516	409.66869759
31	451.88092106	456.55796055	461.28479945	466.06196654	470.88999613
32	518.40365461	523.98714381	529.63238017	535.34004464	541.11082556
33	594.57218453	601.22727323	607.95870767	614.76736118	621.65411692
34	681.78515129	689.70584149	697.72067899	705.83077959	714.03727211
35	781.64399823	791.05804142	800.58789812	810.23498880	820.00075111
36	895.98237797	907.15698645	918.47373125	929.93441466	941.54086152
37	1026.89982278	1040.14832798	1053.57089601	1067.16980641	1080.94736816
38	1176.80029708	1192.48990970	1208.39224683	1224.51018304	1240.84663128
39	1348.43634015	1366.99719156	1385.81751487	1404.90092486	1424.25108608
40	1544.95960948	1566.89528293	1589.14687204	1611.71891035	1634.61599573

i	14.75	14.80	14.85	14.90	14.95
Years					
1	1.00000000	1.00000000	1.00000000	1.00000000	1.00000000
2	2.14750000	2.14800000	2.14850000	2.14900000	2.14950000
3	3.46425625	3.46590400	3.46755225	3.46920100	3.47085025
4	4.97523405	4.97885779	4.98248376	4.98611195	4.98974236
5	6.70908107	6.71572875	6.72238260	6.72904263	6.73570885
6	8.69867053	8.70965660	8.72065641	8.73166998	8.74269732
7	10.98172443	10.99868578	11.01567389	11.03268881	11.04973057
8	13.60152878	13.62649127	13.65150146	13.67655944	13.70166529
9	16.60775428	16.64321198	16.67874943	16.71436680	16.75006425
10	20.05739803	20.10640735	20.15554372	20.20480745	20.25419885
11	24.01586424	24.08215564	24.14864196	24.21532376	24.28220158
12	28.55820422	28.64631468	28.73471529	28.82340700	28.91239072
13	33.77053934	33.88596925	34.00182052	34.11809464	34.23479313
14	39.75169390	39.90109270	40.05109086	40.20169075	40.35289470
15	46.61506874	46.80645441	46.99867786	47.19174267	47.38565246
16	54.49079138	54.73380967	54.97798152	55.22331232	55.46980750
17	63.52818311	63.83441350	64.14221177	64.45158586	64.76254372
18	73.89859012	74.28190670	74.66733022	75.05487215	75.44454401
19	85.79863217	86.27562889	86.75542876	87.23804810	87.72350334
20	99.45393041	100.04442196	100.63860993	101.23651727	101.83816709
21	115.12338515	115.85099641	116.58344350	117.32075835	118.06297307
22	133.10408445	133.99694388	134.89608486	135.80155134	136.71338754
23	153.73693691	154.82849158	155.92815347	157.03598249	158.15203898
24	177.41313511	178.74310833	180.08348426	181.43434388	182.79576881
25	204.58157253	206.19708836	207.82588167	209.46806112	211.12373625
26	235.75735448	237.71425744	239.68802510	241.67880222	243.68673481
27	271.53156427	273.89596754	276.28169682	278.68894376	281.11790167
28	312.58247000	315.43257074	318.30952880	321.21359638	324.14502797
29	359.68838432	363.11659121	366.57849383	370.07442224	373.60470965
30	413.74242101	417.85784671	422.01540016	426.21551115	430.45861374
31	475.76942811	480.70080802	485.68468709	490.72162231	495.81217650
32	546.94541876	552.84452761	558.80886312	564.83914403	570.93609688
33	628.61986803	635.66551769	642.79197929	650.00017650	657.29104337
34	722.34129856	730.74401431	739.24658822	747.85020279	756.55605435
35	829.88664010	839.89412843	850.02470657	860.27988301	870.66118448
36	953.29491951	965.19845944	977.25337549	989.46158558	1001.82503156
37	1094.90592014	1109.04783143	1123.37550176	1137.89136183	1152.59787377
38	1257.40454336	1274.18691048	1291.19676377	1308.43717474	1325.91125590
39	1443.87171351	1463.76657324	1483.93948319	1504.39431378	1525.13498866
40	1657.84279125	1681.40402608	1705.30449644	1729.54906653	1754.14266946

i	15.00	15.05	15.10	15.15	15.20
Years					
1	1.00000000	1.00000000	1.00000000	1.00000000	1.00000000
2	2.15000000	2.15050000	2.15100000	2.15150000	2.15200000
3	3.47250000	3.47415025	3.47580100	3.47745225	3.47910400
4	4.99337500	4.99700986	5.00064695	5.00428627	5.00792781
5	6.74238125	6.74905985	6.75574464	6.76243564	6.76913283
6	8.75373844	8.76479335	8.77586208	8.78694463	8.79804103
7	11.06679920	11.08389475	11.10101726	11.11816675	11.13534326
8	13.72681908	13.75202091	13.77727086	13.80256901	13.82791544
9	16.78584195	16.82170006	16.85763876	16.89365821	16.92975858
10	20.30371824	20.35336592	20.40314221	20.45304743	20.50308189
11	24.34927597	24.41654749	24.48401669	24.55168412	24.61955034
12	29.00166737	29.09123789	29.18110321	29.27126426	29.36172199
13	34.35191748	34.46946919	34.58744979	34.70586080	34.82470373
14	40.50470510	40.65712431	40.81015471	40.96379871	41.11805870
15	47.58041086	47.77602151	47.97248807	48.16981421	48.36800362
16	55.71747249	55.96631275	56.21633377	56.46754107	56.71994017
17	65.07509336	65.38924282	65.70500017	66.02237354	66.34137107
18	75.83635737	76.23032386	76.62645520	77.02476313	77.42525948
19	88.21181097	88.70298761	89.19704993	89.69401474	90.19389892
20	102.44358262	103.05278724	103.66580447	104.28265797	104.90337155
21	118.81012001	119.56223172	120.31934095	121.08148066	121.84868403
22	137.63163801	138.55634759	139.48756143	140.42532498	141.36968400
23	159.27638372	160.40907791	161.55018321	162.69976171	163.85787597
24	184.16784127	185.55064413	186.94426087	188.34877561	189.76427311
25	212.79301747	214.47601607	216.17284426	217.88361512	219.60844263
26	245.71197009	247.75465649	249.81494375	251.89298281	253.98892591
27	283.56876560	286.04173230	288.53700025	291.05476970	293.59524264
28	327.10408044	330.09101301	333.10608729	336.14956731	339.22171952
29	377.16969250	380.76971046	384.40510647	388.07622676	391.78342089
30	434.74514638	439.07555189	443.45027755	447.86977511	452.33450087
31	500.95691834	506.15642245	511.41126946	516.72204604	522.08934500
32	577.10045609	583.33296403	589.63437115	596.00543602	602.44692544
33	664.66552450	672.12457511	679.66916119	687.30025957	695.01885811
34	765.36535317	774.27932367	783.29920453	792.42624890	801.66172454
35	881.17015615	891.80836188	902.57738441	913.47882561	924.51430667
36	1014.34567957	1027.02552034	1039.86656946	1052.87086769	1066.04048128
37	1167.49753151	1182.59286116	1197.88642145	1213.38080414	1229.07863444
38	1343.62216123	1361.57308676	1379.76727109	1398.20799597	1416.89858687
39	1546.16548542	1567.48983632	1589.11212902	1611.03650736	1633.26717208
40	1779.09030823	1804.39705668	1830.06806050	1856.10853823	1882.52378223

i	15.25	15.30	15.35	15.40	15.45
Years					
1	1.00000000	1.00000000	1.00000000	1.00000000	1.00000000
2	2.15250000	2.15300000	2.15350000	2.15400000	2.15450000
3	3.48075625	3.48240900	3.48406225	3.48571600	3.48737025
4	5.01157158	5.01521758	5.01886581	5.02251626	5.02616895
5	6.77583624	6.78254587	6.78926171	6.79598377	6.80271206
6	8.80915127	8.82027538	8.83141338	8.84256527	8.85373107
7	11.15254684	11.16977752	11.18703533	11.20432032	11.22163252
8	13.85331023	13.87875348	13.90424526	13.92978565	13.95537474
9	16.96594004	17.00220276	17.03854690	17.07497264	17.11148014
10	20.55324590	20.60353978	20.65396385	20.70451843	20.75520382
11	24.68761590	24.75588137	24.82434730	24.89301426	24.96188282
12	29.45247732	29.54353122	29.63488461	29.72653846	29.81849371
13	34.94398012	35.06369149	35.18383940	35.30442538	35.42545099
14	41.27293708	41.42843629	41.58455875	41.74130689	41.89868317
15	48.56705999	48.76698705	48.96778852	49.16946815	49.37202972
16	56.97353664	57.22833606	57.48434406	57.74156625	58.00000831
17	66.66200098	66.98427148	67.30819087	67.63376745	67.96100959
18	77.82795612	78.23286502	78.63999817	79.04936764	79.46098557
19	90.69671943	91.20249337	91.71123789	92.22297026	92.73770784
20	105.52796915	106.15647485	106.78891290	107.42530768	108.06568370
21	122.62098444	123.39841550	124.18101103	124.96880506	125.76183184
22	142.32068457	143.27837308	144.24279623	145.21400104	146.19203485
23	165.02458897	166.19996416	167.38406545	168.57695720	169.77870424
24	191.19083878	192.62855867	194.07751949	195.53780861	197.00951404
25	221.34744170	223.10072815	224.86841873	226.65063113	228.44748396
26	256.10292656	258.23513956	260.38572101	262.55482833	264.74262024
27	296.15862285	298.74511591	301.35492918	303.98827189	306.64535506
28	342.32281284	345.45311864	348.61291081	351.80246576	355.02206242
29	395.52704180	399.30744579	403.12499262	406.98004548	410.87297106
30	456.84491567	461.40148500	466.00467899	470.65497249	475.35284509
31	527.51376531	532.99591221	538.53639722	544.13583825	549.79485966
32	608.95961452	615.54428677	622.20173419	628.93275734	635.73816548
33	702.82595574	710.72256265	718.70970039	726.78840197	734.95971205
34	811.00691399	820.46311474	830.03163940	839.71381588	849.51098756
35	935.68546837	946.99397129	958.44149604	970.02974352	981.76043513
36	1079.37750230	1092.88404890	1106.56226569	1120.41432403	1134.44242236
37	1244.98257140	1261.09530838	1277.41957347	1293.95812993	1310.71377662
38	1435.84241354	1455.04289056	1474.50347800	1494.22768194	1514.21905510
39	1655.80838160	1678.66445282	1701.83976187	1725.33874495	1749.16589912
40	1909.31915979	1936.50011410	1964.07216532	1992.04091168	2020.41203053

i	15.50	15.55	15.60	15.65	15.70
Years					
1	1.00000000	1.00000000	1.00000000	1.00000000	1.00000000
2	2.15500000	2.15550000	2.15600000	2.15650000	2.15700000
3	3.48902500	3.49068025	3.49233600	3.49399225	3.49564900
4	5.02982388	5.03348103	5.03714042	5.04080204	5.04446589
5	6.80944658	6.81618733	6.82293432	6.82968756	6.83644704
6	8.86491079	8.87610446	8.88731207	8.89853366	8.90976922
7	11.23897197	11.25633870	11.27373276	11.29115418	11.30860299
8	13.98101262	14.00669937	14.03243507	14.05821980	14.08405366
9	17.14806958	17.18474112	17.22149494	17.25833120	17.29525009
10	20.80602036	20.85696837	20.90804815	20.95926004	21.01060435
11	25.03095352	25.10022695	25.16970366	25.23938423	25.30926923
12	29.91075132	30.00331224	30.09617743	30.18934787	30.28282450
13	35.54691777	35.66882729	35.79118111	35.91398081	36.03722795
14	42.05669003	42.21532993	42.37460537	42.53451880	42.69507274
15	49.57547698	49.77981374	49.98504380	50.19117100	50.39819916
16	58.25967591	58.52057478	58.78271064	59.04608926	59.31071642
17	68.28992568	68.62052415	68.95281350	69.28680223	69.62249890
18	79.87486416	80.29101566	80.70945240	81.13018677	81.55323123
19	93.25546810	93.77626859	94.30012698	94.82706100	95.35708853
20	108.71006566	109.35847836	110.01094678	110.66749605	111.32815143
21	126.56012583	127.36372175	128.17265448	128.98695918	129.80667121
22	147.17694534	148.16878048	149.16758858	150.17341829	151.18631858
23	170.98937187	172.20902584	173.43773240	174.67555826	175.92257060
24	198.49272451	199.98752936	201.49401866	203.01228312	204.54241419
25	230.25909680	232.08559017	233.92708557	235.78370543	237.65557321
26	266.94925681	269.17489945	271.41971091	273.68385533	275.96749821
27	309.32639161	312.03159631	314.76118582	317.51537869	320.29439543
28	358.27198231	361.55250954	364.86393080	368.20653546	371.58061551
29	414.80413957	418.77392477	422.78270401	426.83085826	430.91877215
30	480.09878121	484.89327007	489.73680583	494.62988758	499.57301937
31	555.51409229	561.29417357	567.13574754	573.03946498	579.00598341
32	642.61877660	649.57541756	656.60892416	663.72014125	670.90992281
33	743.22468697	751.58439499	760.03991633	768.59234336	777.24278069
34	859.42451345	869.45576841	879.60614328	889.87704509	900.26989726
35	993.63531304	1005.65614040	1017.82470163	1030.14280265	1042.61227113
36	1148.64878656	1163.03567023	1177.60535508	1192.36015126	1207.30239770
37	1327.68934847	1344.88771695	1362.31179048	1379.96451494	1397.84887413
38	1534.48119749	1555.01775693	1575.83242979	1596.92896152	1618.31114737
39	1773.32578310	1797.82301814	1822.66228884	1847.84834400	1873.38599751
40	2049.19127948	2078.38449746	2107.99760589	2138.03660984	2168.50759912

i	15.75	15.80	15.85	15.90	15.95
Years					
1	1.00000000	1.00000000	1.00000000	1.00000000	1.00000000
2	2.15750000	2.15800000	2.15850000	2.15900000	2.15950000
3	3.49730625	3.49896400	3.50062225	3.50228100	3.50394025
4	5.04813198	5.05180031	5.05547088	5.05914368	5.06281872
5	6.84321277	6.84998476	6.85676301	6.86354752	6.87033831
6	8.92101878	8.93228235	8.94355995	8.95485158	8.96615727
7	11.32607924	11.34358297	11.36111420	11.37867298	11.39625935
8	14.10993672	14.13586907	14.16185080	14.18788199	14.21396272
9	17.33225176	17.36933639	17.40650415	17.44375522	17.48108977
10	21.06208141	21.11369154	21.16543506	21.21731230	21.26932359
11	25.37935923	25.44965480	25.52015652	25.59086496	25.66178070
12	30.37660831	30.47070026	30.56510132	30.65981249	30.75483472
13	36.16092412	36.28507090	36.40966988	36.53472267	36.66023086
14	42.85626967	43.01811210	43.18060256	43.34374358	43.50753768
15	50.60613214	50.81497381	51.02472807	51.23539880	51.44698994
16	59.57659795	59.84373968	60.11214747	60.38182721	60.65278484
17	69.95991213	70.29905054	70.63992284	70.98253774	71.32690402
18	81.97859829	82.40630053	82.83635061	83.26876124	83.70354521
19	95.89022752	96.42649601	96.96591218	97.50849428	98.05426067
20	111.99293835	112.66188238	113.33500926	114.01234487	114.69391524
21	130.63182614	131.46245980	132.29860823	133.14030770	133.98759473
22	152.20633876	153.23352845	154.26793764	155.30961663	156.35861608
23	177.17883711	178.44442594	179.71940575	181.00384567	182.29781535
24	206.08450396	207.63864524	209.20493156	210.78345713	212.37431690
25	239.54281333	241.44555119	243.36391321	245.29802682	247.24802044
26	278.27080643	280.59394828	282.93709346	285.30041308	287.68407970
27	323.09845844	325.92779211	328.78262277	331.66317876	334.56969042
28	374.98646565	378.42438326	381.89466848	385.39762419	388.93355604
29	435.04683399	439.21543582	443.42497344	447.67584643	451.96845823
30	504.56671034	509.61147468	514.70783172	519.85630602	525.05742731
31	585.03596722	591.13008767	597.28902305	603.51345867	609.80408697
32	678.17913205	685.52864153	692.95933321	700.47209860	708.06783884
33	785.99234535	794.84216689	803.79338752	812.84716228	822.00465914
34	910.78613974	921.42722926	932.19463944	943.08986108	954.11440227
35	1055.23495675	1068.01273148	1080.94748979	1094.04114899	1107.29564943
36	1222.43446244	1237.75874305	1253.27766693	1268.99369168	1284.90930552
37	1415.96789028	1434.32462445	1452.92217713	1471.76368866	1490.85233975
38	1639.98283300	1661.94791512	1684.21034221	1706.77411516	1729.64328794
39	1899.28012919	1925.53568571	1952.15768145	1979.15119947	2006.52139236
40	2199.41674954	2230.77032405	2262.57467396	2294.83624018	2327.56155445

i	16.00	16.05	16.10	16.15	16.20
Years					
1	1.00000000	1.00000000	1.00000000	1.00000000	1.00000000
2	2.16000000	2.16050000	2.16100000	2.16150000	2.16200000
3	3.50560000	3.50726025	3.50892100	3.51058225	3.51224400
4	5.06649600	5.07017552	5.07385728	5.07754128	5.08122753
5	6.87713536	6.88393869	6.89074830	6.89756420	6.90438639
6	8.97747702	8.98881085	9.00015878	9.01152082	9.02289698
7	11.41387334	11.43151499	11.44918434	11.46688143	11.48460629
8	14.24009307	14.26627315	14.29250302	14.31878278	14.34511251
9	17.51850797	17.55600999	17.59359601	17.63126620	17.66902074
10	21.32146924	21.37374959	21.42616497	21.47871569	21.53140210
11	25.73290432	25.80423640	25.87577753	25.94752828	26.01948924
12	30.85016901	30.94581634	31.04177771	31.13805409	31.23464650
13	36.78619605	36.91261987	37.03950392	37.16684983	37.29465923
14	43.67198742	43.83709536	44.00286405	44.16929608	44.33639402
15	51.65950541	51.87294916	52.08732516	52.30263740	52.51888986
16	60.92502627	61.19855750	61.47338451	61.74951333	62.02695001
17	71.67303048	72.02092598	72.37059942	72.72205974	73.07531592
18	84.14071536	84.58028460	85.02226593	85.46667239	85.91351709
19	98.60322981	99.15542028	99.71085074	100.26953998	100.83150686
20	115.37974658	116.06986523	116.76429771	117.46307068	118.16621098
21	134.84050604	135.69907860	136.56334964	137.43335660	138.30913715
22	157.41498700	158.47878072	159.55004894	160.62884369	161.71521737
23	183.60138492	184.91462503	186.23760682	187.57040194	188.91308259
24	213.97760651	215.59342234	217.22186151	218.86302186	220.51700197
25	249.21402355	251.19616663	253.19458122	255.20939989	257.24075628
26	290.08826732	292.51315137	294.95890879	297.42571797	299.91375880
27	337.50239009	340.46151217	343.44729311	346.45997142	349.49978773
28	392.50277250	396.10558487	399.74230730	403.41325681	407.11875334
29	456.30321610	460.68053124	465.10081877	469.56449778	474.07199138
30	530.31173068	535.61975651	540.98205060	546.39916417	551.87165398
31	616.16160759	622.58672743	629.08016074	635.64262919	642.27486193
32	715.74746480	723.51189718	731.36206662	739.29891380	747.32338956
33	831.26705917	840.63555668	850.11135935	859.69568838	869.38977867
34	965.26978864	976.55756353	987.97928820	999.53654206	1011.23092282
35	1120.71295482	1134.29505247	1148.04395360	1161.96169360	1176.05033231
36	1301.02702759	1317.34940839	1333.87903013	1350.61850711	1367.57048615
37	1510.19135201	1529.78398844	1549.63355398	1569.74339601	1590.11690490
38	1752.82196833	1776.31431859	1800.12455617	1824.25695447	1848.71584350
39	2034.27348326	2062.41276672	2090.94460972	2119.87445262	2149.20781015
40	2360.75724058	2394.43001578	2428.58669188	2463.23417671	2498.37947539

i	16.25	16.30	16.35	16.40	16.45
Years					
1	1.00000000	1.00000000	1.00000000	1.00000000	1.00000000
2	2.16250000	2.16300000	2.16350000	2.16400000	2.16450000
3	3.51390625	3.51556900	3.51723225	3.51889600	3.52056025
4	5.08491602	5.08860675	5.09229972	5.09599494	5.09969241
5	6.91121487	6.91804965	6.92489073	6.93173811	6.93859181
6	9.03428728	9.04569174	9.05711036	9.06854317	9.07999017
7	11.50235897	11.52013949	11.53794791	11.55578424	11.57364855
8	14.37149230	14.39792223	14.42440239	14.45093286	14.47751373
9	17.70685980	17.74478355	17.78279218	17.82088585	17.85906474
10	21.58422452	21.63718327	21.69027870	21.74351113	21.79688089
11	26.09166100	26.16404415	26.23663927	26.30944695	26.38246780
12	31.33155591	31.42878334	31.52632979	31.62419626	31.72238375
13	37.42293375	37.55167503	37.68088471	37.81056444	37.94071588
14	44.50416048	44.67259806	44.84170936	45.01149701	45.18196364
15	52.73608656	52.95423154	53.17332884	53.39338252	53.61439666
16	62.30570063	62.58577128	62.86716810	63.14989725	63.43396492
17	73.43037698	73.78725200	74.14595009	74.50648040	74.86885214
18	86.36281324	86.81457407	87.26881293	87.72554319	88.18477832
19	101.39677039	101.96534965	102.53726384	103.11253227	103.69117436
20	118.87374558	119.58570164	120.30210648	121.02298756	121.74837254
21	139.19072923	140.07817101	140.97150089	141.87075752	142.77597982
22	162.80922274	163.91091288	165.02034128	166.13756176	167.26262850
23	190.26572143	191.62839168	193.00116708	194.38412189	195.77733089
24	222.18390116	223.86381953	225.55685790	227.26311787	228.98270182
25	259.28878510	261.35362211	263.43540417	265.53426921	267.65035627
26	302.42321268	304.95426251	307.50709275	310.08188936	312.67883987
27	352.56698474	355.66180730	358.78450241	361.93531921	365.11450903
28	410.85911976	414.63468190	418.44576855	422.29271156	426.17584577
29	478.62372672	483.22013504	487.86165171	492.54871626	497.28177240
30	557.40008231	562.98501706	568.62703177	574.32670572	580.08462396
31	648.97759569	655.75157484	662.59755146	669.51628546	676.50854460
32	755.43645499	763.63908153	771.93225113	780.31695628	788.79420019
33	879.19487892	889.11225183	899.14317419	909.28893711	919.55084612
34	1023.06404675	1035.03754887	1047.15308317	1059.41232279	1071.81696030
35	1190.31195435	1204.74866934	1219.36261226	1234.15594373	1249.13085028
36	1384.73764693	1402.12270244	1419.72839937	1437.55751850	1455.61287515
37	1610.75751455	1631.66870294	1652.85399267	1674.31695153	1696.06119311
38	1873.50561067	1898.63070152	1924.09562047	1949.90493159	1976.06325937
39	2178.95027240	2209.10750587	2239.68525441	2270.68934037	2302.12566554
40	2534.02969167	2570.19202932	2606.87379351	2644.08239219	2681.82533752

i	16.50	16.55	16.60	16.65	16.70
Years					
1	1.00000000	1.00000000	1.00000000	1.00000000	1.00000000
2	2.16500000	2.16550000	2.16600000	2.16650000	2.16700000
3	3.52222500	3.52389025	3.52555600	3.52722225	3.52888900
4	5.10339213	5.10709409	5.11079830	5.11450475	5.11821346
5	6.94545183	6.95231816	6.95919081	6.96606980	6.97295511
6	9.09145138	9.10292681	9.11441649	9.12592042	9.13743861
7	11.59154085	11.60946120	11.62740963	11.64538617	11.66339086
8	14.50414509	14.53082703	14.55755962	14.58434296	14.61117714
9	17.89732904	17.93567890	17.97411452	18.01263607	18.05124372
10	21.85038833	21.90403376	21.95781753	22.01173997	22.06580142
11	26.45570240	26.52915135	26.60281524	26.67669468	26.75079026
12	31.82089330	31.91972590	32.01888257	32.11836434	32.21817223
13	38.07134069	38.20244053	38.33401708	38.46607200	38.59860699
14	45.35311190	45.52494444	45.69746391	45.87067299	46.04457436
15	53.83637537	54.05932274	54.28324292	54.50814005	54.73401828
16	63.71937730	64.00614066	64.29426125	64.58374536	64.87459933
17	75.23307456	75.59915694	75.96710861	76.33693897	76.70865742
18	88.64653186	89.11081741	89.57764864	90.04703931	90.51900321
19	104.27320962	104.85865769	105.44753832	106.03987135	106.63567675
20	122.47828921	123.21276554	123.95182968	124.69550993	125.44383477
21	143.68720693	144.60447824	145.52783341	146.45731233	147.39295517
22	168.39559607	169.53651939	170.68545375	171.84245484	173.00757868
23	197.18086942	198.59481334	200.01923907	201.45422357	202.89984432
24	230.71571287	232.46225495	234.22243276	235.99635179	237.78411833
25	269.78380550	271.93475815	274.10335660	276.28974436	278.49406609
26	315.29813340	317.93996062	320.60451379	323.29198680	326.00257512
27	368.32232542	371.55902410	374.82486308	378.12010260	381.44500517
28	430.09550911	434.05204259	438.04579036	442.07709968	446.14632103
29	502.06126811	506.88765564	511.76139156	516.68293678	521.65275665
30	585.90137735	591.77756265	597.71378255	603.71064576	609.76876701
31	683.57510461	690.71674927	697.93427046	705.22846827	712.60015110
32	797.36499687	806.03037127	814.79135935	823.64900824	832.60437633
33	929.93022136	940.42839772	951.04672501	961.78656811	972.64930718
34	1084.36870788	1097.06929754	1109.92048136	1122.92403170	1136.08174147
35	1264.28954468	1279.63426628	1295.16728126	1310.89088298	1326.80739230
36	1473.89731956	1492.41373735	1511.16504995	1530.15421500	1549.38422681
37	1718.09037728	1740.40821089	1763.01844825	1785.92489180	1809.13139269
38	2002.57528954	2029.44576979	2056.67951065	2084.28138628	2112.25633527
39	2334.00021231	2366.31904469	2399.08830942	2432.31423710	2466.00314326
40	2720.11024734	2758.94484658	2798.33696879	2838.29455757	2878.82566819

i	16.75	16.80	16.85	16.90	16.95
Years					
1	1.00000000	1.00000000	1.00000000	1.00000000	1.00000000
2	2.16750000	2.16800000	2.16850000	2.16900000	2.16950000
3	3.53055625	3.53222400	3.53389225	3.53556100	3.53723025
4	5.12192442	5.12563763	5.12935309	5.13307081	5.13679078
5	6.97984676	6.98674475	6.99364909	7.00055978	7.00747681
6	9.14897110	9.16051787	9.17207896	9.18365438	9.19524413
7	11.68142375	11.69948488	11.71757427	11.73569197	11.75383801
8	14.63806223	14.66499833	14.69198553	14.71902391	14.74611356
9	18.08993766	18.12871805	18.16758509	18.20653895	18.24557981
10	22.12000221	22.17434269	22.22882318	22.28344403	22.33820558
11	26.82510258	26.89963226	26.97437989	27.04934608	27.12453143
12	32.31830727	32.41877048	32.51956290	32.62068556	32.72213951
13	38.73162373	38.86512392	38.99910925	39.13358142	39.26854215
14	46.21917071	46.39446474	46.57045916	46.74715668	46.92456005
15	54.96088180	55.18873481	55.41758152	55.64742616	55.87827298
16	65.16682951	65.46044226	65.75544401	66.05184118	66.34964025
17	77.08227345	77.45779656	77.83523633	78.21460234	78.59590427
18	90.99355425	91.47070639	91.95047365	92.43287014	92.91791004
19	107.23497459	107.83778506	108.44412846	109.05402519	109.66749580
20	126.19683283	126.95453295	127.71696410	128.48415545	129.25613633
21	148.33480233	149.28289448	150.23727255	151.19797772	152.16505144
22	174.18088172	175.36242076	176.55225298	177.75043596	178.95702766
23	204.35617941	205.82330744	207.30130760	208.79025963	210.29024385
24	239.58583946	241.40162310	243.23157793	245.07581351	246.93444018
25	280.71646757	282.95709578	285.21609882	287.49362599	289.78982779
26	328.73647589	331.49388787	334.27501147	337.08004879	339.90920360
27	384.79983560	388.18486103	391.60035090	395.04657703	398.52381361
28	450.25380807	454.39991768	458.58501003	462.80944855	467.07360002
29	526.67132092	531.73910385	536.85658422	542.02424536	547.24257522
30	615.88876717	622.07127330	628.31691866	634.62634282	641.00019172
31	720.05013567	727.57924721	735.18831945	742.87819476	750.64972422
32	841.65853340	850.81256074	860.06755128	869.42460967	878.88485248
33	983.63633774	994.74907095	1005.98893367	1017.35736871	1028.85583497
34	1149.39542431	1162.86691486	1176.49806899	1190.29076402	1204.24689900
35	1342.91915789	1359.22855656	1375.73799361	1392.44990314	1409.36674838
36	1568.85811683	1588.57895406	1608.54984554	1628.77393677	1649.25441223
37	1832.64185140	1856.46021835	1880.59049451	1905.03673208	1929.80303510
38	2140.60936151	2169.34553503	2198.46999284	2227.98793980	2257.90464955
39	2500.16142957	2534.79558491	2569.91218663	2605.51790163	2641.61948765
40	2919.93846902	2961.64124318	3003.94239007	3046.85042701	3090.37399081

i	17.00	17.05	17.10	17.15	17.20
Years					
1	1.00000000	1.00000000	1.00000000	1.00000000	1.00000000
2	2.17000000	2.17050000	2.17100000	2.17150000	2.17200000
3	3.53890000	3.54057025	3.54224100	3.54391225	3.54558400
4	5.14051300	5.14423748	5.14796421	5.15169320	5.15542445
5	7.01440021	7.02132997	7.02826609	7.03520858	7.04215745
6	9.20684825	9.21846673	9.23009959	9.24174686	9.25340853
7	11.77201245	11.79021530	11.80844662	11.82670644	11.84499480
8	14.77325456	14.80044701	14.82769100	14.85498660	14.88233391
9	18.28470784	18.32392323	18.36322616	18.40261680	18.44209534
10	22.39310817	22.44815214	22.50333783	22.55866558	22.61413574
11	27.19993656	27.27556208	27.35140860	27.42747673	27.50376709
12	32.82392578	32.92604541	33.02849947	33.13128899	33.23441503
13	39.40399316	39.53993616	39.67637288	39.81330505	39.95073441
14	47.10267200	47.28149527	47.46103264	47.64128686	47.82226073
15	56.11012623	56.34299022	56.57686922	56.81176756	57.04768958
16	66.64884769	66.94947005	67.25151386	67.55498570	67.85989218
17	78.97915180	79.36435469	79.75152272	80.14066574	80.53179364
18	93.40560761	93.89597717	94.38903311	94.88478992	95.38326214
19	110.28456090	110.90524127	111.52955777	112.15753139	112.78918323
20	130.03293626	130.81458491	131.60111215	132.39254802	133.18892275
21	153.13853542	154.11847164	155.10490233	156.09787001	157.09741746
22	180.17208644	181.39567105	182.62784063	183.86865472	185.11817326
23	211.80134114	213.32363296	214.85720138	216.40212900	217.95849907
24	248.80756913	250.69531238	252.59778281	254.51509413	256.44736090
25	292.10485588	294.43886315	296.79200367	299.16443277	301.55630698
26	342.76268138	345.64068931	348.54343630	351.47113299	354.42399178
27	402.03233722	405.57242684	409.14436391	412.74843230	416.38491837
28	471.37783454	475.72252562	480.10805013	484.53478843	489.00312433
29	552.51206642	557.83321623	563.20652671	568.63250465	574.11166171
30	647.43911771	653.94377960	660.51484277	667.15297920	673.85886752
31	758.50376772	766.44119402	774.46288089	782.56971513	790.76259274
32	888.44940823	898.11941760	907.89603352	917.78042128	927.77375869
33	1040.48580763	1052.24877831	1064.14625525	1076.17976353	1088.35084518
34	1218.36839493	1232.65719501	1247.11526490	1261.74459297	1276.54719056
35	1426.49102206	1443.82524676	1461.37197520	1479.13379066	1497.11330733
36	1669.99449581	1690.99745133	1712.26658295	1733.80523576	1755.61679619
37	1954.89356010	1980.31251678	2006.06416864	2032.15283370	2058.58288514
38	2288.22546532	2318.95580089	2350.10114148	2381.66704468	2413.65914138
39	2678.22379443	2715.33776494	2752.96843667	2791.12294284	2829.80851370
40	3134.52183948	3179.30285386	3224.72603934	3270.80052753	3317.53557806

i	17.25	17.30	17.35	17.40	17.45
Years					
1	1.00000000	1.00000000	1.00000000	1.00000000	1.00000000
2	2.17250000	2.17300000	2.17350000	2.17400000	2.17450000
3	3.54725625	3.54892900	3.55060225	3.55227600	3.55395025
4	5.15915795	5.16289372	5.16663174	5.17037202	5.17411457
5	7.04911270	7.05607433	7.06304235	7.07001676	7.07699756
6	9.26508464	9.27677519	9.28848019	9.30019967	9.31193364
7	11.86331174	11.88165730	11.90003151	11.91843441	11.93686605
8	14.90973302	14.93718401	14.96468698	14.99224200	15.01984918
9	18.48166196	18.52131684	18.56106017	18.60089211	18.64081286
10	22.66974865	22.72550466	22.78140410	22.83744734	22.89363471
11	27.58028029	27.65701696	27.73397772	27.81116318	27.88857396
12	33.33787864	33.44168090	33.54582285	33.65030557	33.75513012
13	40.08866271	40.22709169	40.36602311	40.50545874	40.64540033
14	48.00395703	48.18637855	48.36952812	48.55340856	48.73802268
15	57.28463961	57.52262204	57.76164125	58.00170165	58.24280764
16	68.16623995	68.47403566	68.78328601	69.09399773	69.40617758
17	80.92491634	81.32004383	81.71718613	82.11635334	82.51755556
18	95.88446441	96.38841141	96.89511793	97.40459882	97.91686901
19	113.42453452	114.06360658	114.70642089	115.35299901	116.00336265
20	133.99026672	134.79661052	135.60798491	136.42442084	137.24594943
21	158.10358773	159.11642414	160.13597030	161.16227007	162.19536761
22	186.37645661	187.64356552	188.91956114	190.20450506	191.49845926
23	219.52639538	221.10590235	222.69710500	224.30008894	225.91494040
24	258.39469858	260.35722346	262.33505272	264.32830442	266.33709750
25	303.96778409	306.39902312	308.85018437	311.32142938	313.81292101
26	357.40222684	360.40605412	363.43569135	366.49135810	369.57327573
27	420.05411097	423.75630148	427.49178380	431.26085441	435.06381234
28	493.51344511	498.06614164	502.66160829	507.30024307	511.98244760
29	579.64451440	585.23158414	590.87339733	596.57048537	602.32338470
30	680.63319313	687.47664820	694.38993177	701.37374982	708.42881533
31	799.04241895	807.41010833	815.86658493	824.41278229	833.04964361
32	937.87723621	948.09205708	958.41943741	968.86060641	979.41680642
33	1100.66105946	1113.11198295	1125.70520981	1138.44235192	1151.32503914
34	1291.52509222	1306.68035600	1322.01506371	1337.53132116	1353.23125847
35	1515.31317062	1533.73605759	1552.38467726	1571.26177104	1590.37011307
36	1777.70469256	1800.07239555	1822.72341876	1845.66131920	1868.88969780
37	2085.35875202	2112.48491998	2139.96593192	2167.80638874	2196.01095007
38	2446.08313675	2478.94481114	2512.25002111	2546.00470038	2580.21486086
39	2869.03247784	2908.80226347	2949.12539977	2990.00951825	3031.46235408
40	3364.94058026	3413.02505504	3461.79865663	3511.27117443	3561.45253486

i	17.50	17.55	17.60	17.65	17.70
Years					
1	1.00000000	1.00000000	1.00000000	1.00000000	1.00000000
2	2.17500000	2.17550000	2.17600000	2.17650000	2.17700000
3	3.55562500	3.55730025	3.55897600	3.56065225	3.56232900
4	5.17785938	5.18160644	5.18535578	5.18910737	5.19286123
5	7.08398477	7.09097837	7.09797839	7.10498482	7.11199767
6	9.32368210	9.33544508	9.34722259	9.35901464	9.37082126
7	11.95532647	11.97381569	11.99233377	12.01088073	12.02945662
8	15.04750860	15.07522034	15.10298451	15.13080118	15.15867044
9	18.68082260	18.72092152	18.76110978	18.80138759	18.84175511
10	22.94996656	23.00644324	23.06306510	23.11983250	23.17674577
11	27.96621071	28.04407403	28.12216456	28.20048293	28.27902977
12	33.86029758	33.96580902	34.07166552	34.17786817	34.28441804
13	40.78584966	40.92680851	41.06827866	41.21026190	41.35276003
14	48.92337335	49.10946340	49.29629570	49.48387312	49.67219856
15	58.48496368	58.72817422	58.97244374	59.21777673	59.46417770
16	69.71983233	70.03496880	70.35159384	70.66971432	70.98933715
17	82.92080299	83.32610583	83.73347436	84.14291890	84.55444983
18	98.43194351	98.94983740	99.47056585	99.99414409	100.52058745
19	116.65753362	117.31553386	117.97738543	118.64311052	119.31273143
20	138.07260201	138.90441005	139.74140527	140.58361953	141.43108489
21	163.23530736	164.28213402	165.33589260	166.39662837	167.46438691
22	192.80148614	194.11364854	195.43500969	196.76563328	198.10558340
23	227.54174622	229.18059386	230.83157140	232.49476755	234.17027166
24	268.36155181	270.40178808	272.45792797	274.53009403	276.61840974
25	316.32482337	318.85730189	321.41052329	323.98465562	326.57986827
26	372.68166746	375.81675837	378.97877539	382.16794734	385.38450495
27	438.90095927	442.77259946	446.67903986	450.62059005	454.59756233
28	516.70862714	521.47919067	526.29455087	531.15512419	536.06133086
29	608.13263689	613.99878863	619.92239183	625.90400361	631.94418642
30	715.55584835	722.75557604	730.02873279	737.37606025	744.79830742
31	841.77812181	850.59917963	859.51378976	868.52293488	877.62760783
32	990.08929312	1000.87933566	1011.78821676	1022.81723289	1033.96769442
33	1164.35491942	1177.53365907	1190.86294290	1204.34447449	1217.97997633
34	1369.11703032	1385.19081623	1401.45482086	1417.91127424	1434.56243214
35	1609.71251063	1629.29180448	1649.11086933	1669.17261415	1689.47998263
36	1892.41219998	1916.23251617	1940.35438233	1964.78158054	1989.51793955
37	2224.58433498	2253.53132276	2282.85675362	2312.56552951	2342.66261485
38	2614.88659360	2650.02606990	2685.63954225	2721.73334547	2758.31389768
39	3073.49174748	3116.10564517	3159.31210169	3203.11928094	3247.53545757
40	3612.35280329	3663.98218589	3716.35103159	3769.46983403	3823.34923356

i	17.75	17.80	17.85	17.90	17.95
Years					
1	1.00000000	1.00000000	1.00000000	1.00000000	1.00000000
2	2.17750000	2.17800000	2.17850000	2.17900000	2.17950000
3	3.56400625	3.56568400	3.56736225	3.56904100	3.57072025
4	5.19661736	5.20037575	5.20413641	5.20789934	5.21166453
5	7.11901694	7.12604264	7.13307476	7.14011332	7.14715832
6	9.38264245	9.39447823	9.40632861	9.41819361	9.43007324
7	12.04806148	12.06669535	12.08535826	12.10405026	12.12277138
8	15.18659240	15.21456712	15.24259471	15.27067526	15.29880885
9	18.88221255	18.92276007	18.96339787	19.00412613	19.04494503
10	23.23380527	23.29101136	23.34836439	23.40586470	23.46351267
11	28.35780571	28.43681138	28.51604743	28.59551449	28.67521319
12	34.39131622	34.49856381	34.60616190	34.71411158	34.82241396
13	41.49577485	41.63930817	41.78336180	41.92793755	42.07303727
14	49.86127489	50.05110502	50.24169188	50.43303838	50.62514746
15	59.71165118	59.96020172	60.20983388	60.46055224	60.71236142
16	71.31046926	71.63311762	71.95728922	72.28299110	72.61023030
17	84.96807756	85.38381256	85.80166535	86.22164650	86.64376664
18	101.04991132	101.58213119	102.11726261	102.65532123	103.19632275
19	119.98627058	120.66375054	121.34519399	122.03062373	122.72006268
20	142.28383361	143.14189814	144.00531112	144.87410537	145.74831393
21	168.53921408	169.62115601	170.71025915	171.80657023	172.91013628
22	199.45492458	200.81372178	202.18204041	203.55994631	204.94750575
23	235.85817369	237.55856426	239.27153462	240.99717669	242.73558303
24	278.72299952	280.84398870	282.98150355	285.13567132	287.30662018
25	329.19633193	331.83421868	334.49370194	337.17495649	339.87815851
26	388.62868085	391.90070961	395.20082774	398.52927370	401.88628796
27	458.61027170	462.65903592	466.74417549	470.86601369	475.02487665
28	541.01359493	546.01234431	551.05801081	556.15103015	561.29184200
29	638.04350803	644.20254160	650.42186574	656.70206454	663.04372764
30	752.29623070	759.87059401	767.52216877	775.25173410	783.06007676
31	886.82881165	896.12755974	905.52487590	915.02179450	924.61936053
32	1045.24092572	1056.63826537	1068.16106625	1079.81069571	1091.58853575
33	1231.77119004	1245.71987661	1259.82781657	1274.09681025	1288.52867792
34	1451.41057627	1468.45801464	1485.70708183	1503.16013928	1520.81957560
35	1710.03595356	1730.84354125	1751.90579594	1773.22580421	1794.80668942
36	2014.56733531	2039.93369159	2065.62098052	2091.63322317	2117.97449017
37	2373.15303733	2404.04188870	2435.33432554	2467.03557011	2499.15091116
38	2795.38770146	2832.96134488	2871.04150265	2909.63493716	2948.74849971
39	3292.56901847	3338.22846427	3384.52241087	3431.45959091	3479.04885541
40	3878.00001925	3933.43313091	3989.65966121	4046.69085769	4104.53812496

i	18.00	18.05	18.10	18.15	18.20
Years					
1	1.00000000	1.00000000	1.00000000	1.00000000	1.00000000
2	2.18000000	2.18050000	2.18100000	2.18150000	2.18200000
3	3.57240000	3.57408025	3.57576100	3.57744225	3.57912400
4	5.21543200	5.21920174	5.22297374	5.22674802	5.23052457
5	7.15420976	7.16126765	7.16833199	7.17540278	7.18248004
6	9.44196752	9.45387646	9.46580008	9.47773839	9.48969141
7	12.14152167	12.16030116	12.17910989	12.19794791	12.21681524
8	15.32699557	15.35523552	15.38352878	15.41187545	15.44027562
9	19.08585477	19.12685553	19.16794749	19.20913085	19.25040578
10	23.52130863	23.57925295	23.63734599	23.69558809	23.75397963
11	28.75514419	28.83530811	28.91570561	28.99633733	29.07720392
12	34.93107014	35.04008123	35.14944833	35.25917256	35.36925504
13	42.21866276	42.36481589	42.51149848	42.65871238	42.80645945
14	50.81802206	51.01166515	51.20607970	51.40126868	51.59723508
15	60.96526603	61.19927071	61.47438012	61.73059894	61.98793186
16	72.93901392	73.26934908	73.60124293	73.93470265	74.26973546
17	87.06803642	87.49446659	87.92306790	88.35385118	88.78682731
18	103.74028298	104.28721781	104.83714319	105.39007517	105.94602988
19	123.41353392	124.11106062	124.81266610	125.51837381	126.22820732
20	146.62797002	147.51310706	148.40375867	149.29995866	150.20174105
21	174.02100463	175.13922289	176.26483899	177.39790116	178.53845792
22	206.34478546	207.75185262	209.16877484	210.59562022	212.03245726
23	244.48684684	246.25106202	248.02832309	249.81872528	251.62236449
24	289.49447928	291.69937871	293.92144957	296.16082392	298.41763482
25	342.60348554	345.35111657	348.12123194	350.91401347	353.72964436
26	405.27211294	408.68699311	412.13117492	415.60490691	419.10843963
27	479.22109327	483.45499536	487.72691759	492.03719751	496.38617565
28	566.48089006	571.71862203	577.00548967	582.34194886	587.72845961
29	669.44745027	675.91383330	682.44348330	689.03701258	695.69503926
30	790.94799132	798.91628021	806.96575378	815.09723036	823.31153641
31	934.31862976	944.12066879	954.02655521	964.03737767	974.15423604
32	1103.49598312	1115.53444951	1127.70536170	1140.01016172	1152.45030700
33	1303.12526008	1317.88841764	1332.82003217	1347.92200608	1363.19626287
34	1538.68780689	1556.76727703	1575.06045799	1593.56985018	1612.29798271
35	1816.65161213	1838.76377053	1861.14640089	1883.80277799	1906.73621557
36	2144.64890232	2171.66063111	2199.01389945	2226.71298219	2254.76220680
37	2531.68570473	2564.64537503	2598.03541525	2631.86138846	2666.12892844
38	2988.38913158	3028.56386522	3069.27982541	3110.54423046	3152.36439341
39	3527.29917527	3576.21964289	3625.81947381	3676.10800829	3727.09471301
40	4163.21302682	4222.72728844	4283.09279857	4344.32161180	4406.42595078

i	18.25	18.30	18.35	18.40	18.45
Years					
1	1.00000000	1.00000000	1.00000000	1.00000000	1.00000000
2	2.18250000	2.18300000	2.18350000	2.18400000	2.18450000
3	3.58080625	3.58248900	3.58417225	3.58585600	3.58754025
4	5.23430339	5.23808449	5.24186786	5.24565350	5.24944143
5	7.18956376	7.19665395	7.20375061	7.21085375	7.21796337
6	9.50165915	9.51364162	9.52563885	9.53765084	9.54967761
7	12.23571194	12.25463804	12.27359358	12.29257859	12.31159313
8	15.46872937	15.49723680	15.52579800	15.55441305	15.58308206
9	19.29177248	19.33323113	19.37478193	19.41642506	19.45816070
10	23.81252096	23.87121243	23.93005441	23.98904727	24.04819135
11	29.15830603	29.23964430	29.32121940	29.40303196	29.48508266
12	35.47969688	35.59049921	35.70166316	35.81318984	35.92508041
13	42.95474156	43.10356057	43.25291835	43.40281678	43.55325774
14	51.79398190	51.99151215	52.18982886	52.38893506	52.58883380
15	62.24638359	62.50595887	62.76666246	63.02849911	63.29147363
16	74.60634860	74.94454935	75.28434502	75.62574295	75.96875052
17	89.22200722	89.65940188	90.09902233	90.54087965	90.98498499
18	106.50502353	107.06707242	107.63219293	108.20040151	108.77171472
19	126.94219033	127.66034668	128.38270033	129.10927539	129.84009608
20	151.10914006	152.02219012	152.94092584	153.86538206	154.79559381
21	179.68655813	180.84225091	182.00558573	183.17661236	184.35538087
22	213.47935498	214.93638283	216.40361071	217.88110903	219.36894864
23	253.43933727	255.26974088	257.11367328	258.97123309	260.84251966
24	300.69201632	302.98410347	305.29403233	307.62193998	309.96796454
25	356.56830930	359.43019440	362.31548726	365.22437694	368.15705400
26	422.64202574	426.20591997	429.80037917	433.42566230	437.08203046
27	500.77419544	505.20160333	509.66874875	514.17598416	518.72366508
28	593.16548611	598.65349674	604.19296414	609.78436524	615.42818129
29	702.41818732	709.20708664	716.06237306	722.98468845	729.97468074
30	831.60950651	839.99198350	848.45981852	857.01387112	865.65500933
31	984.37824145	994.71051648	1005.15219522	1015.70442341	1026.36835855
32	1165.02727051	1177.74254099	1190.59762304	1203.59403732	1216.73332071
33	1378.64474738	1394.26942600	1410.07228687	1426.05534018	1442.22061838
34	1631.24741378	1650.42073095	1669.82055151	1689.44952278	1709.31032247
35	1929.95006680	1953.44772472	1977.23262271	2001.30823497	2025.67807696
36	2283.16595399	2311.92865834	2341.05480898	2370.54895020	2400.41568216
37	2700.84374059	2736.01160282	2771.63836643	2807.72995704	2844.29237552
38	3194.74772325	3237.70172613	3281.23400666	3325.35226913	3370.06431880
39	3778.78918274	3831.20114201	3884.34044689	3938.21708665	3992.84118562
40	4469.41820859	4533.31095100	4598.11691889	4663.84903060	4730.52038437

i	18.50	18.55	18.60	18.65	18.70
Years					
1	1.00000000	1.00000000	1.00000000	1.00000000	1.00000000
2	2.18500000	2.18550000	2.18600000	2.18650000	2.18700000
3	3.58922500	3.59091025	3.59259600	3.59428225	3.59596900
4	5.25323163	5.25702410	5.26081886	5.26461589	5.26841520
5	7.22507948	7.23220207	7.23933116	7.24646675	7.25360885
6	9.56171918	9.57377556	9.58584676	9.59793280	9.61003370
7	12.33063723	12.34971092	12.36881426	12.38794727	12.40711000
8	15.61180511	15.64058230	15.66941371	15.69829944	15.72723957
9	19.49998906	19.54191031	19.58392466	19.62603228	19.66823337
10	24.10748704	24.16693468	24.22653464	24.28628730	24.34619301
11	29.56737214	29.64990106	29.73267009	29.81567988	29.89893111
12	36.03733598	36.14995771	36.26294673	36.37630418	36.49003122
13	43.70424314	43.85577486	44.00785482	44.16048491	44.31366706
14	52.78952812	52.99102110	53.19331581	53.39641535	53.60032280
15	63.55559082	63.82085551	64.08727255	64.35484681	64.62358317
16	76.31337512	76.65962421	77.00750525	77.35702574	77.70819322
17	91.43134952	91.87998450	92.33090122	92.78411104	93.23962535
18	109.34614918	109.92372163	110.50444885	111.08834775	111.67543529
19	130.57518678	131.31457199	132.05827634	132.80632460	133.55874169
20	155.73159634	156.67342509	157.62111574	158.57470414	159.53422639
21	185.54194166	186.73634545	187.93864326	189.14888646	190.36712672
22	220.86720087	222.37593753	223.89523091	225.42515379	226.96577942
23	262.72763303	264.62667394	266.53974386	268.46694497	270.40838017
24	312.33224514	314.71492196	317.11613622	319.53603021	321.97474726
25	371.11371049	374.09453998	377.09973756	380.12949984	383.18402500
26	440.76974693	444.48907715	448.24028874	452.02365156	455.83943768
27	523.31215011	527.94180096	532.61298245	537.32606258	542.08141252
28	621.12489788	626.87500503	632.67899718	638.53737325	644.45063667
29	737.03300399	744.16031847	751.35729066	758.62459336	765.96290572
30	874.38410973	883.20205754	892.10974672	901.10808002	910.19796909
31	1037.14517003	1048.03603922	1059.04215961	1070.16473694	1081.40498931
32	1230.01702649	1243.44672449	1257.02400130	1270.75046039	1284.62772231
33	1458.57017639	1475.10609189	1491.83046554	1508.74542125	1525.85310639
34	1729.40565902	1749.73827193	1770.31093213	1791.12644231	1812.18763728
35	2050.34570594	2075.31472138	2100.58876551	2126.17152380	2152.06672545
36	2430.65966153	2461.28560219	2492.29827589	2523.70251299	2555.50320311
37	2881.33169892	2918.85408140	2956.86575521	2995.37303166	3034.38230209
38	3415.37806322	3461.30151350	3507.84278568	3555.01010207	3602.81179258
39	4048.22300491	4104.37294425	4161.30154381	4219.01948610	4277.53759780
40	4798.14426082	4866.73412541	4936.30363096	5006.86662026	5078.43712859

i	18.75	18.80	18.85	18.90	18.95
Years					
1	1.00000000	1.00000000	1.00000000	1.00000000	1.00000000
2	2.18750000	2.18800000	2.18850000	2.18900000	2.18950000
3	3.59765625	3.59934400	3.60103225	3.60272100	3.60441025
4	5.27221680	5.27602067	5.27982683	5.28363527	5.28744599
5	7.26075745	7.26791256	7.27507419	7.28224233	7.28941701
6	9.62214947	9.63428012	9.64642567	9.65858614	9.67076153
7	12.42630249	12.44552478	12.46477691	12.48405892	12.50337084
8	15.75623421	15.78528344	15.81438736	15.84354605	15.87275962
9	19.71052812	19.75291673	19.79539937	19.83797625	19.88064756
10	24.40625215	24.46646507	24.52683216	24.58735377	24.64803028
11	29.98242443	30.06616051	30.15014002	30.23436363	30.31883201
12	36.60412901	36.71859868	36.83344141	36.94865835	37.06425068
13	44.46740319	44.62169523	44.77654512	44.93195478	45.08792618
14	53.80504129	54.01057394	54.21692387	54.42409424	54.63208819
15	64.89348653	65.16456184	65.43681402	65.71024805	65.98486891
16	78.06101526	78.41549946	78.77165346	79.12948493	79.48900157
17	93.69745562	94.15761336	94.62011014	95.08495758	95.55216736
18	112.26572855	112.85924467	113.45600090	114.05601456	114.65930308
19	134.31555265	135.07678267	135.84245707	136.61260132	137.38724101
20	160.49971878	161.47121781	162.44876023	163.43238297	164.42212318
21	191.59341605	192.82780676	194.07035153	195.32110335	196.58011553
22	228.51718155	230.07943443	231.65261280	233.23679188	234.83204742
23	272.36415310	274.33436811	276.31913031	278.31854554	280.33272040
24	324.43243180	326.90922931	329.40528637	331.92075065	334.45577092
25	386.26351277	389.36816442	392.49818285	395.65377252	398.83513951
26	459.68792141	463.56937934	467.48409032	471.43233553	475.41439845
27	546.87940667	551.72042265	556.60484135	561.53304695	566.50542695
28	650.41929542	656.44386211	662.52485394	668.66279282	674.85820536
29	773.37291332	780.85530818	788.41078891	796.04006066	803.74383527
30	919.38033456	928.65610612	938.02622262	947.49163213	957.05329206
31	1092.76414729	1104.24345407	1115.84416558	1127.56755060	1139.41489090
32	1298.65742491	1312.84122344	1327.18079079	1341.67781766	1356.33401273
33	1543.15569208	1560.65537345	1578.35436986	1596.25492520	1614.35930814
34	1833.49738435	1855.05858366	1876.87416858	1898.94710606	1921.28039703
35	2178.27814391	2204.80959738	2231.66494935	2258.84810911	2286.36303227
36	2587.70529589	2620.31380169	2653.33379231	2686.77040173	2720.62882689
37	3073.90003887	3113.93279641	3154.48721216	3195.57000766	3237.18798958
38	3651.25629616	3700.35216213	3750.10805165	3800.53273911	3851.63511361
39	4336.86685169	4397.01836862	4458.00341938	4519.83342680	4582.51996763
40	5151.02938639	5224.65782192	5299.33706394	5375.08194446	5451.90750150

i	19.00	19.05	19.10	19.15	19.20
Years					
1	1.00000000	1.00000000	1.00000000	1.00000000	1.00000000
2	2.19000000	2.19050000	2.19100000	2.19150000	2.19200000
3	3.60610000	3.60779025	3.60948100	3.61117225	3.61286400
4	5.29125900	5.29507429	5.29889187	5.30271174	5.30653389
5	7.29659821	7.30378595	7.31098022	7.31818103	7.32538839
6	9.68295187	9.69515717	9.70737744	9.71961270	9.73186297
7	12.52271273	12.54208461	12.56148653	12.58091853	12.60038066
8	15.90202814	15.93135173	15.96073046	15.99016443	16.01965374
9	19.92341349	19.96627423	20.00922998	20.05228092	20.09542726
10	24.70886205	24.76984947	24.83099290	24.89229272	24.95374929
11	30.40354584	30.48850580	30.57371255	30.65916677	30.74486916
12	37.18021955	37.29656615	37.41329164	37.53039721	37.64788404
13	45.24446127	45.40156200	45.55923035	45.71746828	45.87627777
14	54.84090891	55.05055956	55.26104334	55.47236345	55.68452310
15	66.26068160	66.53769116	66.81590262	67.09532105	67.37595154
16	79.85021111	80.21312132	80.57774002	80.94407503	81.31213424
17	96.02175122	96.49372094	96.96808836	97.44486540	97.92406401
18	115.26588395	115.87577477	116.48899324	117.10555713	117.72548430
19	138.16640190	138.95010987	139.73839095	140.53127132	141.32877728
20	165.41801826	166.42010580	167.42842362	168.44300977	169.46390252
21	197.84744173	199.12313595	200.40725253	201.69984615	203.00097181
22	236.43845566	238.05609335	239.68503777	241.32536668	242.97715839
23	282.36176223	284.40577914	286.46487998	288.53917440	290.62877281
24	337.01049706	339.58508006	342.17967206	344.79442630	347.42949718
25	402.04249150	405.27603782	408.53598942	411.82255894	415.13596064
26	479.43056488	483.48112302	487.56636340	491.68657897	495.84206509
27	571.52237221	576.58427695	581.69153881	586.84455885	592.04374158
28	681.11162293	687.42358171	693.79462273	700.22529187	706.71613997
29	811.52283129	819.37777403	827.30939567	835.31843526	843.40563884
30	966.71216923	976.46923998	986.32549024	996.28191561	1006.33952150
31	1151.38748139	1163.48663020	1175.71365887	1188.06990245	1200.55670963
32	1371.15110285	1386.13083325	1401.27496772	1416.58528877	1432.06359788
33	1632.66981239	1651.18875699	1669.91848655	1688.86137157	1708.01980867
34	1943.87707675	1966.74021520	1989.87291748	2013.27832422	2036.95961194
35	2314.21372133	2342.40422619	2370.93864472	2399.82112331	2429.05585743
36	2754.91432838	2789.63223128	2824.78792587	2860.38686843	2896.43458205
37	3279.34805077	3322.05717134	3365.32241971	3409.15095373	3453.55002181
38	3903.42418042	3955.90906248	4009.09900187	4063.00336137	4117.63162599
39	4646.07477470	4710.50973888	4775.83691123	4842.06850507	4909.21689818
40	5529.82898189	5608.86184414	5689.02176127	5770.32462380	5852.78654264

i	19.25	19.30	19.35	19.40	19.45
Years					
1	1.00000000	1.00000000	1.00000000	1.00000000	1.00000000
2	2.19250000	2.19300000	2.19350000	2.19400000	2.19450000
3	3.61455625	3.61624900	3.61794225	3.61963600	3.62133025
4	5.31035833	5.31418506	5.31801408	5.32184538	5.32567898
5	7.33260231	7.33982277	7.34704980	7.35428339	7.36152355
6	9.74412825	9.75640857	9.76870394	9.78101437	9.79333988
7	12.61987294	12.63939542	12.65894815	12.67853115	12.69814448
8	16.04919848	16.07879874	16.10845461	16.13816620	16.16793358
9	20.13866919	20.18200689	20.22544058	20.26897044	20.31259666
10	25.01536300	25.07713423	25.13906333	25.20115070	25.26339672
11	30.83082038	30.91702113	31.00347209	31.09017394	31.17712738
12	37.76575331	37.88400621	38.00264394	38.12166768	38.24107865
13	46.03566082	46.19561941	46.35615554	46.51727122	46.67896845
14	55.89752553	56.11137395	56.32607163	56.54162183	56.75802781
15	67.65779919	67.94086913	68.22516650	68.51069647	68.79746422
16	81.68192553	82.05345687	82.42673621	82.80177158	83.17857102
17	98.40569620	98.88977404	99.37630967	99.86531527	100.35680308
18	118.34879272	118.97550043	119.60562559	120.23918643	120.87620128
19	142.13093532	142.93777202	143.74931414	144.56558860	145.38662243
20	170.49114036	171.52476202	172.56480643	173.61131278	174.66432049
21	204.31068488	205.62904109	206.95609648	208.29190747	209.63653082
22	244.64049172	246.31544601	248.00210114	249.70053751	251.41083607
23	292.73378638	294.85432710	296.99050771	299.14244179	301.31024368
24	350.08504026	352.76121223	355.45817096	358.17607550	360.91508608
25	418.47641051	421.84412618	425.23932704	428.66223414	432.11307032
26	500.03311953	504.26004254	508.52313682	512.82270757	517.15906250
27	597.28949504	602.58223075	607.92236379	613.31031284	618.74650015
28	713.26772284	719.88060128	726.55534119	733.29251353	740.09269443
29	851.57175948	859.81755733	868.14379971	876.55126115	885.04072350
30	1016.49932318	1026.76234590	1037.12962495	1047.60220582	1058.18114422
31	1213.17544289	1225.92747865	1238.81420738	1251.83703374	1264.99737677
32	1447.71171565	1463.53148203	1479.52475651	1495.69341829	1512.03936655
33	1727.39622091	1746.99305807	1766.81279689	1786.85794144	1807.13102334
34	2060.91999344	2085.16271827	2109.69107309	2134.50838208	2159.61800739
35	2458.64709218	2488.59912290	2518.91629573	2549.60300820	2580.66370982
36	2932.93665742	2969.89875362	3007.32659896	3045.22599179	3083.60280138
37	3498.52696397	3544.08921307	3590.24429585	3636.99983420	3684.36354625
38	4172.99340454	4229.09843119	4285.95656710	4343.57780204	4401.97225600
39	4977.29463491	5046.31442841	5116.28916283	5187.23189563	5259.15585979
40	5936.42385213	6021.25311309	6107.29111584	6194.55488338	6283.06167452

i	19.50	19.55	19.60	19.65	19.70
Years					
1	1.00000000	1.00000000	1.00000000	1.00000000	1.00000000
2	2.19500000	2.19550000	2.19600000	2.19650000	2.19700000
3	3.62302500	3.62472025	3.62641600	3.62811225	3.62980900
4	5.32951488	5.33335306	5.33719354	5.34103631	5.34488137
5	7.36877028	7.37602358	7.38328347	7.39054994	7.39782300
6	9.80568048	9.81803619	9.83040703	9.84279300	9.85519414
7	12.71778817	12.73746227	12.75716681	12.77690183	12.79666738
8	16.19775687	16.22763614	16.25757150	16.28756304	16.31761085
9	20.35631946	20.40013901	20.44405551	20.48806918	20.53218019
10	25.32580175	25.38836618	25.45109040	25.51397477	25.57701969
11	31.26433309	31.35179177	31.43950411	31.52747081	31.61569257
12	38.36087804	38.48106706	38.60164692	38.72261883	38.84398400
13	46.84124926	47.00411567	47.16756972	47.33161343	47.49624885
14	56.97529287	57.19342029	57.41241338	57.63227547	57.85300988
15	69.08547498	69.37473395	69.66524640	69.95701760	70.25005282
16	83.55714260	83.93749444	84.31963470	84.70357155	85.08931323
17	100.85078540	101.34727460	101.84628310	102.34782336	102.85190794
18	121.51668856	122.16066679	122.80815459	123.45917065	124.11373380
19	146.21244283	147.04307715	147.87855288	148.71889769	149.56413936
20	175.72386918	176.78999873	177.86274925	178.94216108	180.02827481
21	210.99002367	212.35244348	213.72384810	215.10429574	216.49384495
22	253.13307828	254.86734618	256.61372233	258.37228985	260.14313240
23	303.49402855	305.69391236	307.91001191	310.14244480	312.39132949
24	363.67536411	366.45707223	369.26037424	372.08543521	374.93242140
25	435.59206012	439.09942985	442.63540759	446.20022323	449.79410841
26	521.53251184	525.94336838	530.39194748	534.87856709	539.40354777
27	624.23135165	629.76529690	635.34876919	640.98220552	646.66604668
28	746.95646522	753.88441244	760.87712795	767.93520891	775.05925787
29	893.61297593	902.26881507	911.00904503	919.83447746	928.74593167
30	1068.86750624	1079.66236842	1090.56681785	1101.58195228	1112.70888021
31	1278.29666996	1291.73636145	1305.31791415	1319.04280590	1332.91252961
32	1528.56452060	1545.27082011	1562.16022533	1579.23471727	1596.49629795
33	1827.63460212	1848.37126544	1869.34362949	1890.55433921	1912.00606864
34	2185.02334953	2210.72784784	2236.73498087	2263.04826686	2289.67126417
35	2612.10290269	2643.92514209	2676.13503712	2708.73725130	2741.73650321
36	3122.46296871	3161.81250737	3201.65750440	3242.00412118	3282.85859434
37	3732.34324761	3780.94685256	3830.18237526	3880.05793099	3930.58173743
38	4461.15018090	4521.12196223	4581.89812081	4643.48931443	4705.90633970
39	5332.07446617	5406.00130585	5480.95015249	5556.93496472	5633.96988862
40	6372.82898707	6463.87456115	6556.21638237	6649.87268529	6744.86195668

i	19.75	19.80	19.85	19.90	19.95
Years					
1	1.00000000	1.00000000	1.00000000	1.00000000	1.00000000
2	2.19750000	2.19800000	2.19850000	2.19900000	2.19950000
3	3.63150625	3.63320400	3.63490225	3.63660100	3.63830025
4	5.34872873	5.35257839	5.35643035	5.36028460	5.36414115
5	7.40510266	7.41238891	7.41968177	7.42698123	7.43428731
6	9.86761043	9.88004192	9.89248860	9.90495050	9.91742763
7	12.81646350	12.83629022	12.85614759	12.87603565	12.89595444
8	16.34771504	16.37787568	16.40809289	16.43836674	16.46869735
9	20.57638876	20.62069507	20.66509932	20.70960173	20.75420247
10	25.64022553	25.70359269	25.76712154	25.83081247	25.89466586
11	31.70417008	31.79290404	31.88189516	31.97114415	32.06065170
12	38.96574367	39.08789904	39.21045136	39.33340184	39.45675172
13	47.66147804	47.82730305	47.99372595	48.16074880	48.32837369
14	58.07461996	58.29710906	58.52048055	58.74473781	58.96988424
15	70.54435740	70.83993665	71.13679594	71.43494064	71.73437614
16	85.47686798	85.86624411	86.25744993	86.65049382	87.04538418
17	103.35854941	103.86776044	104.37955375	104.89394210	105.41093833
18	124.77186292	125.43357701	126.09889516	126.76783657	127.44042052
19	150.41430584	151.26942526	152.12952585	152.99463605	153.86478442
20	181.12113125	182.22077146	183.32723674	184.44056862	185.56080891
21	217.89255467	219.30048421	220.71769323	222.14424178	223.58019029
22	261.92633422	263.72198008	265.53015533	267.35094589	269.18443825
23	314.65678523	316.93893213	319.23789117	321.55378413	323.88673368
24	377.80150031	380.69284070	383.60661256	386.54298717	389.50213705
25	453.41729662	457.07002315	460.75252516	464.46504162	468.20781339
26	543.96721270	548.56988774	553.21190140	557.89358490	562.61527216
27	652.40073721	658.18672551	664.02446383	669.91440829	675.85701896
28	782.24988281	789.50769716	796.83331990	804.22737554	811.69049424
29	937.74423466	946.83022120	956.00473390	965.26862328	974.62274784
30	1123.94872101	1135.30260500	1146.77167358	1158.35707931	1170.05998604
31	1346.92859341	1361.09252079	1375.40585078	1389.87013809	1404.48695325
32	1613.94699061	1631.58883991	1649.42391216	1667.45429557	1685.68210043
33	1933.70152125	1955.64343021	1977.83455873	2000.27770039	2022.97567946
34	2316.60757170	2343.86082939	2371.43471863	2399.33296276	2427.55932751
35	2775.13756711	2808.94527361	2843.16451028	2877.80022235	2912.85741335
36	3324.22723661	3366.11643778	3408.53266557	3451.48246660	3494.97246731
37	3981.76211585	4033.60749246	4086.12639969	4139.32747746	4193.21947454
38	4769.16013373	4833.26177597	4898.22249003	4964.05364547	5030.76675972
39	5712.06926014	5791.24760761	5871.51965430	5952.90032092	6035.40472828
40	6841.20293901	6938.91463392	7038.01630568	7138.52748478	7240.46797157

i	20.00	20.05	20.10	20.15	20.20
Years					
1	1.00000000	1.00000000	1.00000000	1.00000000	1.00000000
2	2.20000000	2.20050000	2.20100000	2.20150000	2.20200000
3	3.64000000	3.64170025	3.64340100	3.64510225	3.64680400
4	5.36800000	5.37186115	5.37572460	5.37959035	5.38345841
5	7.44160000	7.44891931	7.45624525	7.46357781	7.47091701
6	9.92992000	9.94242763	9.95495054	9.96748874	9.98004224
7	12.91590400	12.93588437	12.95589560	12.97593772	12.99601077
8	16.49908480	16.52952919	16.56003061	16.59058917	16.62120495
9	20.79890176	20.84369979	20.88859677	20.93359289	20.97868835
10	25.95868211	26.02286160	26.08720472	26.15171185	26.21638340
11	32.15041853	32.24044535	32.33073287	32.42128179	32.51209284
12	39.58050224	39.70465464	39.82921017	39.95417007	40.07953560
13	48.49660269	48.66543790	48.83488142	49.00493534	49.17560179
14	59.19592323	59.42285820	59.65069258	59.87942981	60.10907335
15	72.03510787	72.33714127	72.64048179	72.94513492	73.25110617
16	87.44212945	87.84073809	88.24121863	88.64357961	89.04782961
17	105.93055534	106.45280608	106.97770358	107.50526090	108.03549120
18	128.11666640	128.79659370	129.48022199	130.16757097	130.85866042
19	154.73999969	155.62031074	156.50574661	157.39633652	158.29210982
20	186.68799962	187.82218304	188.96340168	190.11169833	191.26711601
21	225.02559955	226.48053074	227.94504542	229.41920555	230.90307344
22	271.03071946	272.88987715	274.76199955	276.64717546	278.54549428
23	326.23686335	328.60429752	330.98916146	333.39158132	335.81168412
24	392.48423602	395.48945917	398.51798292	401.56998496	404.64564431
25	471.98108322	475.78509574	479.62009748	483.48633692	487.38406446
26	567.37729986	572.18000743	577.02373708	581.90883381	586.83564548
27	681.85275984	687.90209892	694.00550823	700.16346383	706.37644587
28	819.22331180	826.82646976	834.50061538	842.24640179	850.06448794
29	984.06797417	993.60517694	1003.23523908	1012.95905175	1022.77751450
30	1181.88156900	1193.82301492	1205.88552213	1218.07030068	1230.37857243
31	1419.25788280	1434.18452941	1449.26851208	1464.51146626	1479.91504406
32	1704.10945936	1722.73852756	1741.57148301	1760.61052672	1779.85788296
33	2045.93135123	2069.14760233	2092.62735109	2116.37354785	2140.38917532
34	2456.11762148	2485.01169660	2514.24544866	2543.82281774	2573.74778874
35	2948.34114577	2984.25654177	3020.60878384	3057.40311551	3094.64484206
36	3539.00937493	3583.59997839	3628.75114939	3674.46984329	3720.76310016
37	4247.81124991	4303.11177406	4359.13013042	4415.87551671	4473.35724639
38	5098.37349989	5166.88568476	5236.31528663	5306.67443333	5377.97541016
39	6119.04819987	6203.84626456	6289.81465925	6376.96933165	6465.32644301
40	7343.85783985	7448.71744060	7555.06740576	7662.92865198	7772.32238450

i	20.25	20.30	20.35	20.40	20.45
Years					
1	1.00000000	1.00000000	1.00000000	1.00000000	1.00000000
2	2.20250000	2.20300000	2.20350000	2.20400000	2.20450000
3	3.64850625	3.65020900	3.65191225	3.65361600	3.65532025
4	5.38732877	5.39120143	5.39507639	5.39895366	5.40283324
5	7.47826284	7.48561532	7.49297444	7.50034021	7.50771264
6	9.99261107	10.00519523	10.01779474	10.03040961	10.04303987
7	13.01611481	13.03624986	13.05641597	13.07661318	13.09684153
8	16.65187806	16.68260858	16.71339662	16.74424226	16.77514562
9	21.02388336	21.06917812	21.11457283	21.16006769	21.20566290
10	26.28121974	26.34622128	26.41138840	26.47672149	26.54222096
11	32.60316674	32.69450420	32.78610594	32.87797268	32.97010515
12	40.20530800	40.33148855	40.45807849	40.58507910	40.71249165
13	49.34688288	49.51878072	49.69129747	49.86443524	50.03819620
14	60.33962666	60.57109321	60.80347650	61.03678003	61.27100732
15	73.55840106	73.86702513	74.17698397	74.48828316	74.80092831
16	89.45397727	89.86203123	90.27200021	90.68389292	91.09771815
17	108.56840767	109.10402357	109.64235225	110.18340708	110.72720152
18	131.55351022	132.25214036	132.95457093	133.66082212	134.37091423
19	159.19309604	160.09932485	161.01082612	161.92762983	162.84976619
20	192.42969799	193.59948780	194.77652923	195.96086632	197.15254337
21	232.39671183	233.90018382	235.41355293	236.93688305	238.47023849
22	280.45704597	282.38192114	284.32021095	286.27200719	288.23740226
23	338.24959778	340.70545113	343.17937388	345.67149666	348.18195102
24	407.74514133	410.86865771	414.01637646	417.18848198	420.38516001
25	491.31353245	495.27499522	499.26870907	503.29493230	507.35392523
26	591.80452278	596.81581925	601.86989137	606.96709849	612.10780294
27	712.64493864	718.96943056	725.35041426	731.78838658	738.28384864
28	857.95553871	865.92022497	873.95922356	882.07321745	890.26289568
29	1032.69153530	1042.70203063	1052.80992556	1063.01615381	1073.32165785
30	1242.81157120	1255.37054285	1268.05674541	1280.87144918	1293.81593688
31	1495.48091437	1511.21076305	1527.10629310	1543.16922482	1559.40129597
32	1799.31579953	1818.98654795	1838.87242375	1858.97574668	1879.29886100
33	2164.67724894	2189.24081719	2214.08296198	2239.20679900	2264.61547808
34	2604.02439185	2634.65670308	2665.64884474	2697.00498600	2728.72934334
35	3132.33933119	3170.49201380	3209.10838465	3248.19400314	3287.75449406
36	3767.63804576	3815.10189260	3863.16194092	3911.82557979	3961.10028809
37	4531.58475003	4590.56757680	4650.31539590	4710.83799806	4772.14529700
38	5450.23066191	5523.45279489	5597.65457897	5672.84894967	5749.04901024
39	6554.90237095	6645.71371225	6737.77728579	6831.11013540	6925.72953284
40	7883.27010106	7995.79359584	8109.91496345	8225.65660302	8343.04122230

i	20.50	20.55	20.60	20.65	20.70
Years					
1	1.00000000	1.00000000	1.00000000	1.00000000	1.00000000
2	2.20500000	2.20550000	2.20600000	2.20650000	2.20700000
3	3.65702500	3.65873025	3.66043600	3.66214225	3.66384900
4	5.40671513	5.41059932	5.41448582	5.41837462	5.42226574
5	7.51509173	7.52247748	7.52986989	7.53726898	7.54467475
6	10.05568553	10.06834660	10.08102309	10.09371503	10.10642243
7	13.11710106	13.13739182	13.15771385	13.17806718	13.19845187
8	16.80610678	16.83712584	16.86820290	16.89933806	16.93053140
9	21.25135867	21.29715520	21.34305270	21.38905137	21.43515140
10	26.60788720	26.67372060	26.73972156	26.80589047	26.87222775
11	33.06250407	33.15517018	33.24810420	33.34130686	33.43477889
12	40.84031741	40.96855765	41.09721366	41.22628672	41.35577812
13	50.21258248	50.38759625	50.56323968	50.73951493	50.91642419
14	61.50616189	61.74224728	61.97926705	62.21722476	62.45612400
15	75.11492507	75.43027909	75.74699606	76.06508168	76.38454166
16	91.51348471	91.93120145	92.35087725	92.77252104	93.19614179
17	111.27374908	111.82306335	112.37515796	112.93004664	113.48774314
18	135.08486764	135.80270286	136.52444050	137.25010127	137.97970597
19	163.77726551	164.71015830	165.64847525	166.59224718	167.54150510
20	198.35160493	199.55809583	200.77206115	201.99354622	203.22259666
21	240.01368395	241.56728453	243.13110574	244.70521351	246.28967417
22	290.21648916	292.20936150	294.21611353	296.23684011	298.27163672
23	350.71086943	353.25838529	355.82463291	358.40974759	361.01386552
24	423.60659767	426.85298346	430.12450730	433.42136046	436.74373569
25	511.44595019	515.57127156	519.73015580	523.92287140	528.14968897
26	617.29236998	622.52116787	627.79456789	633.11294434	638.47667459
27	744.83730582	751.44926787	758.12024888	764.85076735	771.64134623
28	898.52895352	906.87209242	915.29302015	923.79245081	932.37110490
29	1083.72738899	1094.23430741	1104.84338230	1115.55559190	1126.37192361
30	1306.89150373	1320.09945758	1333.44111905	1346.91782163	1360.53091180
31	1575.80426199	1592.37989611	1609.12998958	1626.05635180	1643.16081055
32	1899.84413570	1920.61396476	1941.61076743	1962.83698844	1984.29509833
33	2290.31218352	2316.30013452	2342.58258552	2369.16282656	2396.04418368
34	2760.82618114	2793.29981217	2826.15459813	2859.39495024	2893.02532970
35	3327.79554827	3368.32292357	3409.34244535	3450.86000746	3492.88157295
36	4010.99363567	4061.51328436	4112.66698909	4164.46259900	4216.90805855
37	4834.24733098	4897.15426430	4960.87638885	5025.42412570	5090.80802668
38	5826.26803383	5904.51946561	5983.81692495	6064.17420766	6145.60528820
39	7021.65298077	7118.89821579	7217.48321149	7317.42618154	7418.74558285
40	8462.09184183	8582.83179914	8705.28475305	8829.47468802	8955.42591850

i	20.75	20.80	20.85	20.90	20.95
Years					
1	1.00000000	1.00000000	1.00000000	1.00000000	1.00000000
2	2.20750000	2.20800000	2.20850000	2.20900000	2.20950000
3	3.66555625	3.66726400	3.66897225	3.67068100	3.67239025
4	5.42615917	5.43005491	5.43395296	5.43785333	5.44175601
5	7.55208720	7.55950633	7.56693216	7.57436467	7.58180389
6	10.11914529	10.13188365	10.14463751	10.15740689	10.17019181
7	13.21886794	13.23931545	13.25979443	13.28030493	13.30084699
8	16.96178304	16.99309306	17.02446157	17.05588866	17.08737443
9	21.48135302	21.52765642	21.57406181	21.62056939	21.66717938
10	26.93873377	27.00540896	27.07225370	27.13926840	27.20645346
11	33.52852103	33.62253402	33.71681859	33.81137549	33.90620546
12	41.48568915	41.61602110	41.74677527	41.87795297	42.00955550
13	51.09396964	51.27215348	51.45097791	51.63044514	51.81055738
14	62.69596834	62.93676141	63.17850681	63.42120817	63.66486915
15	76.70538178	77.02760778	77.35122548	77.67624068	78.00265923
16	93.62174849	94.04935020	94.47895599	94.91057499	95.34421634
17	114.04826131	114.61161504	115.17781832	115.74688516	116.31882967
18	138.71327553	139.45083097	140.19239344	140.93798416	141.68762448
19	168.49628020	169.45660381	170.42250747	171.39402284	172.37118181
20	204.45925834	205.70357741	206.95560027	208.21537362	209.48294440
21	247.88455445	249.48992151	251.10584293	252.73238670	254.36962125
22	300.32059950	302.38382518	304.46141118	306.55345553	308.66005690
23	363.63712389	366.27966082	368.94161541	371.62312773	374.32433883
24	440.09182710	443.46583027	446.86594223	450.29236143	453.74528781
25	532.41088122	536.70672297	541.03749118	545.40346496	549.80492561
26	643.88613907	649.34172135	654.84380809	660.39278914	665.98905752
27	778.49251293	785.40479939	792.37874208	799.41488207	806.51376507
28	941.02970936	949.76899766	958.58970980	967.49259243	976.47839885
29	1137.29337406	1148.32094917	1159.45566429	1170.69854424	1182.05062341
30	1374.28174918	1388.17170660	1402.20217030	1416.37453999	1430.69022902
31	1660.44521213	1677.91142157	1695.56132281	1713.39681885	1731.41983200
32	2005.98759365	2027.91699726	2050.08585861	2072.49675399	2095.15228680
33	2423.23001933	2450.72373269	2478.52876013	2506.64857557	2535.08669089
34	2927.05024834	2961.47426909	2996.30200662	3031.53812787	3067.18735263
35	3535.41317487	3578.46091706	3622.03097500	3666.12959659	3710.76310301
36	4270.01140865	4323.78078781	4378.22443329	4433.35068228	4489.16797309
37	5157.03877595	5224.12719167	5292.08422763	5360.92097487	5430.64866345
38	6228.12432196	6311.74564754	6396.48378909	6482.35345862	6569.36955844
39	7521.46011876	7625.58874223	7731.15065911	7838.16533148	7946.65248093
40	9083.16309341	9212.71120061	9344.09557154	9477.34188575	9612.47617569

i	21.00	21.05	21.10	21.15	21.20
Years					
1	1.0000000	1.0000000	1.0000000	1.0000000	1.0000000
2	2.2100000	2.2105000	2.2110000	2.2115000	2.2120000
3	3.6741000	3.6758103	3.6775210	3.6792323	3.6809440
4	5.4456610	5.4495683	5.4534779	5.4573899	5.4613041
5	7.5892498	7.5967024	7.6041618	7.6116278	7.6191006
6	10.1829923	10.1958083	10.2086399	10.2214871	10.2343499
7	13.3214206	13.3420259	13.3626629	13.3833316	13.4040321
8	17.1189190	17.1505224	17.1821848	17.2139063	17.2456869
9	21.7138920	21.7607074	21.8076258	21.8546475	21.9017726
10	27.2738093	27.3413363	27.4090348	27.4769054	27.5449483
11	34.0013092	34.0966876	34.1923412	34.2882709	34.3844774
12	42.1415842	42.2740403	42.4069252	42.5402402	42.6739866
13	51.9913168	52.1727258	52.3547864	52.5375010	52.7208717
14	63.9094934	64.1550846	64.4016463	64.6491824	64.8976966
15	78.3304870	78.6597299	78.9903937	79.3224845	79.6560082
16	95.7798893	96.2176030	96.6573668	97.0991900	97.5430820
17	116.8936660	117.4714084	118.0520712	118.6356687	119.2222153
18	142.4413359	143.1991399	143.9610582	144.7271126	145.4973250
19	173.3540164	174.3425588	175.3368415	176.3368969	177.3427579
20	210.7583598	212.0416675	213.3329150	214.6321506	215.9394226
21	256.0176154	257.6764385	259.3461601	261.0268505	262.7185801
22	310.7813147	312.9173288	315.0681999	317.2340294	319.4149191
23	377.0453907	379.7864265	382.5475901	385.3290266	388.1308820
24	457.2249228	460.7314692	464.2651316	467.8261157	471.4146290
25	554.2421566	558.7154435	563.2250743	567.7713392	572.3545303
26	671.6330094	677.3250444	683.0655650	688.8549774	694.6936907
27	813.6759414	820.9019662	828.1923993	835.5478051	842.9687532
28	985.5478891	994.7018301	1003.9409955	1013.2661659	1022.6781289
29	1193.5129459	1205.0865654	1216.7725455	1228.5719600	1240.4858922
30	1445.1506645	1459.7572874	1474.5115527	1489.4149295	1504.4689013
31	1749.6323040	1768.0361964	1786.6334903	1805.4261871	1824.4163084
32	2118.0550879	2141.2078157	2164.6131567	2188.2738257	2212.1925658
33	2563.8466563	2592.9320609	2622.3465328	2652.0937398	2682.1773897
34	3103.2544541	3139.7442597	3176.6616512	3214.0115657	3251.7989964
35	3755.9378895	3801.6604264	3847.9372596	3894.7750119	3942.1803836
36	4545.6848463	4602.9099461	4660.8520214	4719.5199269	4778.9226249
37	5501.2786640	5572.8224898	5645.2917979	5718.6983915	5793.0542214
38	6657.5471835	6746.9016239	6837.4483672	6929.2031013	7022.1817163
39	8056.6320920	8168.1244157	8281.1499727	8395.7295572	8511.8842402
40	9749.5248314	9888.5146052	10029.4726169	10172.4263585	10317.4036991

i	21.25	21.30	21.35	21.40	21.45
Years					
1	1.0000000	1.0000000	1.0000000	1.0000000	1.0000000
2	2.2125000	2.2130000	2.2135000	2.2140000	2.2145000
3	3.6826563	3.6843690	3.6860823	3.6877960	3.6895103
4	5.4652207	5.4691396	5.4730608	5.4769843	5.4809102
5	7.6265801	7.6340663	7.6415593	7.6490590	7.6565654
6	10.2472284	10.2601225	10.2730322	10.2859576	10.2988987
7	13.4247644	13.4455285	13.4663246	13.4871525	13.5080125
8	17.2775268	17.3094261	17.3413849	17.3734032	17.4054812
9	21.9490013	21.9963339	22.0437705	22.0913115	22.1389569
10	27.6131641	27.6815530	27.7501156	27.8188521	27.8877631
11	34.4809614	34.5777238	34.6747652	34.7720865	34.8696883
12	42.8081657	42.9427790	43.0778276	43.2133130	43.3492365
13	52.9049010	53.0895909	53.2749438	53.4609620	53.6476477
14	65.1471924	65.3976737	65.6491443	65.9016078	66.1550682
15	79.9909708	80.3273782	80.6652366	81.0045519	81.3453303
16	97.9890521	98.4371098	98.8872646	99.3395260	99.7939036
17	119.8117257	120.4042142	120.9996956	121.5981846	122.1996959
18	146.2717174	147.0503118	147.8331306	148.6201961	149.4115307
19	178.3544573	179.3720283	180.3955040	181.4249181	182.4603041
20	217.2547795	218.5782703	219.9099441	221.2498506	222.5980393
21	264.4214201	266.1354418	267.8607172	269.5973186	271.3453187
22	321.6109719	323.8222910	326.0489803	328.2911447	330.5488896
23	390.9533034	393.7964389	396.6604376	399.5454497	402.4516264
24	475.0308804	478.6750804	482.3474411	486.0481760	489.7775002
25	576.9749425	581.6328725	586.3286197	591.0624856	595.8347740
26	700.5821178	706.5206744	712.5097801	718.5498575	724.6413330
27	850.4558178	858.0095780	865.6306181	873.3195270	881.0768990
28	1032.1776791	1041.7656182	1051.4427551	1061.2099058	1071.0678938
29	1252.5154359	1264.6616948	1276.9257833	1289.3088257	1301.8119570
30	1519.6749660	1535.0346358	1550.5494380	1566.2209144	1582.0506218
31	1843.6058962	1862.9970133	1882.5917430	1902.3921900	1922.4004802
32	2236.3721492	2260.8153771	2285.5250801	2310.5041187	2335.7553832
33	2712.6012309	2743.3690524	2774.4846848	2805.9520001	2837.7749129
34	3290.0289925	3328.7066606	3367.8371649	3407.4257281	3447.4776317
35	3990.1601534	4038.7211793	4087.8703997	4137.6148340	4187.9615838
36	4839.0691859	4899.9687905	4961.6307300	5024.0644084	5087.2793435
37	5868.3713880	5944.6621428	6021.9388908	6100.2141918	6179.5007626
38	7116.4003079	7211.8751793	7308.6228440	7406.6600289	7506.0036762
39	8629.6353733	8749.0045925	8870.0138212	8992.6852751	9117.0414648
40	10464.4328902	10613.5425706	10764.7617721	10918.1199240	11073.6468590

i	21.50	21.55	21.60	21.65	21.70
Years					
1	1.0000000	1.0000000	1.0000000	1.0000000	1.0000000
2	2.2150000	2.2155000	2.2160000	2.2165000	2.2170000
3	3.6912250	3.6929403	3.6946560	3.6963723	3.6980890
4	5.4848384	5.4887689	5.4927017	5.4966368	5.5005743
5	7.6640786	7.6715986	7.6791253	7.6866587	7.6941989
6	10.3118555	10.3248281	10.3378163	10.3508203	10.3638401
7	13.5289045	13.5498285	13.5707846	13.5917729	13.6127934
8	17.4376189	17.4698165	17.5020741	17.5343918	17.5667696
9	22.1867070	22.2345620	22.2825221	22.3305876	22.3787586
10	27.9568490	28.0261101	28.0955469	28.1651598	28.2349492
11	34.9675715	35.0657369	35.1641851	35.2629169	35.3619332
12	43.4855994	43.6224031	43.7596490	43.8973384	44.0354727
13	53.8350033	54.0230310	54.2117332	54.4011122	54.5911702
14	66.4095290	66.6649942	66.9214676	67.1789530	67.4374542
15	81.6875777	82.0313005	82.3765046	82.7231963	83.0713817
16	100.2504070	100.7090457	101.1698296	101.6327683	102.0978716
17	122.8042445	123.4118451	124.0225128	124.6362626	125.2531097
18	150.2071570	151.0070977	151.8113755	152.6200135	153.4330345
19	183.5016958	184.5491272	185.6026326	186.6622464	187.7280030
20	223.9545604	225.3194642	226.6928013	228.0746227	229.4649796
21	273.1047908	274.8758087	276.6584464	278.4527785	280.2588802
22	332.8223209	335.1115455	337.4166708	339.7378051	342.0750572
23	405.3791199	408.3280835	411.2986717	414.2910399	417.3053447
24	493.5356306	497.3227855	501.1391848	504.9850500	508.8606044
25	600.6457912	605.4958458	610.3852487	615.3143134	620.2833556
26	730.7846363	736.9802005	743.2284624	749.5298622	755.8848438
27	888.9033331	896.7994337	904.7658103	912.8030774	920.9118549
28	1081.0175497	1091.0597117	1101.1952253	1111.4249436	1121.7497274
29	1314.4363229	1327.1830796	1340.0533940	1353.0484439	1366.1694182
30	1598.0401324	1614.1910332	1630.5049271	1646.9834320	1663.6281820
31	1942.6187608	1963.0492009	1983.6939913	2004.5553451	2025.6354975
32	2361.2817944	2387.0863037	2413.1718934	2439.5415773	2466.1984004
33	2869.9573802	2902.5034021	2935.4170224	2968.7023287	3002.3634533
34	3487.9982170	3528.9928853	3570.4670993	3612.4263829	3654.8763227
35	4238.9178336	4290.4908521	4342.6879927	4395.5166948	4448.9844847
36	5151.2851678	5216.0916307	5281.7085991	5348.1460592	5415.4141179
37	6259.8114789	6341.1593771	6423.5576565	6507.0196811	6591.5589815
38	7606.6709469	7708.6792229	7812.0461103	7916.7894420	8022.9272805
39	9243.1052005	9370.8995955	9500.4480702	9631.7743562	9764.9025003
40	11231.3728186	11391.3284583	11553.5448533	11718.0535043	11884.8863429

i	21.75	21.80	21.85	21.90	21.95
Years					
1	1.0000000	1.0000000	1.0000000	1.0000000	1.0000000
2	2.2175000	2.2180000	2.2185000	2.2190000	2.2195000
3	3.6998063	3.7015240	3.7032423	3.7049610	3.7066803
4	5.5045141	5.5084562	5.5124007	5.5163475	5.5202966
5	7.7017459	7.7092997	7.7168602	7.7244276	7.7320017
6	10.3768757	10.3899270	10.4029942	10.4160772	10.4291760
7	13.6338461	13.6549311	13.6760484	13.6971981	13.7183802
8	17.5992077	17.6317061	17.6642650	17.6968845	17.7295646
9	22.4270353	22.4754180	22.5239069	22.5725022	22.6212040
10	28.3049155	28.3750592	28.4453806	28.5158801	28.5865583
11	35.4612346	35.5608221	35.6606962	35.7608579	35.8613079
12	44.1740532	44.3130813	44.4525583	44.5924858	44.7328650
13	54.7819097	54.9733330	55.1654423	55.3582402	55.5517288
14	67.6969751	67.9575196	68.2190915	68.4816948	68.7453333
15	83.4210672	83.7722588	84.1249630	84.4791859	84.8349340
16	102.5651493	103.0346113	103.5062674	103.9801276	104.4562020
17	125.8730692	126.4961565	127.1223868	127.7517756	128.3843383
18	154.2504618	155.0723186	155.8986283	156.7294144	157.5647005
19	188.7999372	189.8780841	190.9624786	192.0531562	193.1501523
20	230.8639236	232.2715064	233.6877802	235.1127974	236.5466107
21	282.0768270	283.9066948	285.7485602	287.6025000	289.4685918
22	344.4285369	346.7983543	349.1846206	351.5874475	354.0069477
23	420.3417436	423.4003955	426.4814602	429.5850985	432.7114727
24	512.7660729	516.7016817	520.6676592	524.6642351	528.6916410
25	625.2926937	630.3426483	635.4335428	640.5657026	645.7394562
26	762.2938546	768.7573457	775.2757718	781.8495915	788.4792668
27	929.0927679	937.3464470	945.6735280	954.0746520	962.5504658
28	1132.1704450	1142.6879725	1153.3031939	1164.0170008	1174.8302931
29	1379.4175168	1392.7939505	1406.2999417	1419.9367240	1433.7055424
30	1680.4408267	1697.4230317	1714.5764790	1731.9028666	1749.4039090
31	2046.9367065	2068.4612526	2090.2114396	2112.1895943	2134.3980670
32	2493.1454401	2520.3858057	2547.9226392	2575.7591155	2603.8984427
33	3036.4045733	3070.8299113	3105.6437359	3140.8503618	3176.4541509
34	3697.8225680	3741.2708320	3785.2268921	3829.6965910	3874.6858371
35	4503.0989766	4557.8678734	4613.2989681	4669.4001445	4726.1793783
36	5483.5230040	5552.4830698	5622.3047926	5692.9987761	5764.5757518
37	6677.1892573	6763.9243790	6851.7783898	6940.7655081	7030.9001293
38	8130.4779208	8239.4598936	8349.8919680	8461.7931543	8575.1827077
39	9899.8568686	10036.6621504	10175.3433630	10315.9258551	10458.4353121
40	12054.0757375	12225.6544992	12399.6558878	12576.1136174	12755.0618631

i	22.00	22.05	22.10	22.15	22.20
Years					
1	1.0000000	1.0000000	1.0000000	1.0000000	1.0000000
2	2.2200000	2.2205000	2.2210000	2.2215000	2.2220000
3	3.7084000	3.7101203	3.7118410	3.7135623	3.7152840
4	5.5242480	5.5282018	5.5321579	5.5361163	5.5400770
5	7.7395826	7.7471703	7.7547647	7.7623660	7.7699742
6	10.4422907	10.4554213	10.4685678	10.4817301	10.4949084
7	13.7395947	13.7608417	13.7821212	13.8034333	13.8247781
8	17.7623055	17.7951073	17.8279700	17.8608938	17.8938788
9	22.6700127	22.7189284	22.7679514	22.8170818	22.8663199
10	28.6574155	28.7284522	28.7996687	28.8710654	28.9426429
11	35.9620469	36.0630759	36.1643954	36.2660064	36.3679097
12	44.8736973	45.0149841	45.1567268	45.2989269	45.4415856
13	55.7459107	55.9407881	56.1363635	56.3326392	56.5296176
14	69.0100110	69.2757319	69.5424998	69.8103187	70.0791927
15	85.1922134	85.5510307	85.9113922	86.2733043	86.6367735
16	104.9345004	105.4150330	105.8978099	106.3828413	106.8701372
17	129.0200905	129.6590478	130.3012259	130.9466406	131.5953077
18	158.4045104	159.2488678	160.0977968	160.9513215	161.8094660
19	194.2535027	195.3632432	196.4794099	197.6020392	198.7311675
20	237.9892733	239.4408383	240.9013595	242.3708909	243.8494866
21	291.3469134	293.2375431	295.1405600	297.0560432	298.9840727
22	356.4432343	358.8964214	361.3666237	363.8539568	366.3585368
23	435.8607459	439.0330823	442.2286475	445.4476082	448.6901320
24	532.7501099	536.8398770	540.9611787	545.1142534	549.2993413
25	650.9551341	656.2130698	661.5135991	666.8570605	672.2437951
26	795.1652636	801.9080517	808.7081045	815.5658994	822.4819176
27	971.1016216	979.7287771	988.4325956	997.2137461	1006.0729033
28	1185.7439784	1196.7589725	1207.8761993	1219.0965909	1230.4210878
29	1447.6076536	1461.6443259	1475.8168393	1490.1264858	1504.5745693
30	1767.0813375	1784.9368998	1802.9723608	1821.1895024	1839.5901237
31	2156.8392317	2179.5154862	2202.4292526	2225.5829772	2248.9791311
32	2632.3438627	2661.0986509	2690.1661174	2719.5496067	2749.2524982
33	3212.4595124	3248.8709034	3285.6928293	3322.9298445	3360.5865528
34	3920.2006052	3966.2469376	4012.8309446	4059.9588051	4107.6367676
35	4783.6447383	4841.8043874	4900.6665834	4960.2396804	5020.5321299
36	5837.0465808	5910.4222548	5984.7138983	6059.9327696	6136.0902628
37	7122.1968285	7214.6703620	7308.3356698	7403.2078781	7499.3023011
38	8690.0801308	8806.5051768	8924.4778528	9044.0184231	9165.1474120
39	10602.8977596	10749.3395683	10897.7874583	11048.2685038	11200.8101375
40	12936.5352667	13120.5689431	13307.1984866	13496.4599774	13688.3899880

i	22.25	22.30	22.35	22.40	22.45
Years					
1	1.0000000	1.0000000	1.0000000	1.0000000	1.0000000
2	2.2225000	2.2230000	2.2235000	2.2240000	2.2245000
3	3.7170063	3.7187290	3.7204523	3.7221760	3.7239003
4	5.5440401	5.5480056	5.5519733	5.5559434	5.5599159
5	7.7775891	7.7852108	7.7928394	7.8004748	7.8081170
6	10.5081026	10.5213128	10.5345390	10.5477811	10.5610392
7	13.8461555	13.8675656	13.8890084	13.9104841	13.9319925
8	17.9269251	17.9600327	17.9932018	18.0264325	18.0597249
9	22.9156659	22.9651200	23.0146824	23.0643534	23.1141331
10	29.0144016	29.0863418	29.1584639	29.2307685	29.3032560
11	36.4701059	36.5725960	36.6753806	36.7784607	36.8818369
12	45.5847045	45.7282849	45.8723282	46.0168359	46.1618093
13	56.7273012	56.9256924	57.1247935	57.3246071	57.5251355
14	70.3491257	70.6201218	70.8921849	71.1653191	71.4395284
15	87.0018062	87.3684089	87.7365882	88.1063506	88.4777026
16	107.3597081	107.8515641	108.3457157	108.8421731	109.3409468
17	132.2472432	132.9024629	133.5609831	134.2228199	134.8879893
18	162.6722548	163.5397122	164.4118629	165.2887315	166.1703429
19	199.8668314	201.0090680	202.1579142	203.3134074	204.4755849
20	245.3372014	246.8340902	248.3402080	249.8556106	251.3803537
21	300.9247288	302.8780923	304.8442445	306.8232674	308.8152432
22	368.8804809	371.4199068	373.9769332	376.5516793	379.1442652
23	451.9563879	455.2465461	458.5607778	461.8992554	465.2621528
24	553.5166842	557.7665259	562.0491116	566.3646887	570.7135061
25	677.6741465	683.1484611	688.6670880	694.2303789	699.8386882
26	829.4566441	836.4905679	843.5841822	850.7379838	857.9524737
27	1015.0107474	1024.0279646	1033.1252469	1042.3032922	1051.5628041
28	1241.8506387	1253.3862007	1265.0287396	1276.7792296	1288.6386536
29	1519.1624058	1533.8913235	1548.7626629	1563.7777770	1578.9380313
30	1858.1760410	1876.9490886	1895.9111181	1915.0639991	1934.4096193
31	2272.6202102	2296.5087353	2320.6472529	2345.0383349	2369.6845789
32	2779.2782069	2809.6301833	2840.3119140	2871.3269219	2902.6787668
33	3398.6676080	3437.1777142	3476.1216267	3515.5041524	3555.3301500
34	4155.8711508	4204.6683445	4254.0348103	4303.9770825	4354.5017687
35	5081.5524818	5143.3093853	5205.8115904	5269.0679490	5333.0874157
36	6213.1979090	6291.2673782	6370.3104809	6450.3391696	6531.3655406
37	7596.6344437	7695.2200035	7795.0748734	7896.2151436	7998.6571044
38	9287.8856075	9412.2540643	9538.2741076	9665.9673357	9795.3556244
39	11355.4401551	11512.1867207	11671.0783706	11832.1440189	11995.4129620
40	13883.0255897	14080.4043594	14280.5643864	14483.5442791	14689.3831720

i	22.50	22.55	22.60	22.65	22.70
Years					
1	1.0000000	1.0000000	1.0000000	1.0000000	1.0000000
2	2.2250000	2.2255000	2.2260000	2.2265000	2.2270000
3	3.7256250	3.7273503	3.7290760	3.7308023	3.7325290
4	5.5638906	5.5678677	5.5718472	5.5758290	5.5798131
5	7.8157660	7.8234219	7.8310846	7.8387542	7.8464307
6	10.5743134	10.5876035	10.6009098	10.6142320	10.6275704
7	13.9535339	13.9751081	13.9967154	14.0183556	14.0400289
8	18.0930790	18.1264950	18.1599730	18.1935132	18.2271155
9	23.1640218	23.2140197	23.2641270	23.3143439	23.3646707
10	29.3759267	29.4487811	29.5218196	29.5950428	29.6684509
11	36.9855102	37.0894812	37.1937509	37.2983200	37.4031893
12	46.3072500	46.4531592	46.5995386	46.7463894	46.8937132
13	57.7263812	57.9283467	58.1310343	58.3344466	58.5385861
14	71.7148170	71.9911888	72.2686481	72.5471988	72.8268452
15	88.8506508	89.2252019	89.6013625	89.9791393	90.3585390
16	109.8420472	110.3454849	110.8512705	111.3594144	111.8699274
17	135.5565079	136.2283918	136.9036576	137.5823217	138.2644009
18	167.0567221	167.9478941	168.8438842	169.7447176	170.6504199
19	205.6444846	206.8201443	208.0026020	209.1918962	210.3880652
20	252.9144936	254.4580868	256.0111901	257.5738607	259.1461560
21	310.8202547	312.8383854	314.8697190	316.9143401	318.9723334
22	381.7548120	384.3834413	387.0302755	389.6954381	392.3790531
23	468.6496447	472.0619073	475.4991178	478.9614549	482.4490982
24	575.0958148	579.5118674	583.9619184	588.4462244	592.9650435
25	705.4923731	711.1917935	716.9373120	722.7292942	728.5681083
26	865.2281570	872.5655429	879.9651445	887.4274793	894.9530689
27	1060.9044924	1070.3290728	1079.8372672	1089.4298034	1099.1074155
28	1300.6080032	1312.6882787	1324.8804896	1337.1856539	1349.6047989
29	1594.2448039	1609.6994856	1625.3034802	1641.0582045	1656.9650882
30	1953.9498847	1973.6867196	1993.6220667	2013.7578878	2034.0961632
31	2394.5886088	2419.7530749	2445.1806538	2470.8740494	2496.8359923
32	2934.3710458	2966.4073932	2998.7914816	3031.5270216	3064.6177626
33	3595.6045311	3636.3322604	3677.5183564	3719.1678919	3761.2859947
34	4405.6155506	4457.3251851	4509.6375050	4562.5594195	4616.0979154
35	5397.8790495	5463.4520144	5529.8155811	5596.9791280	5664.9521422
36	6613.4018356	6696.4604436	6780.5539024	6865.6949005	6951.8962785
37	8102.4172486	8207.5122737	8313.9590844	8421.7747954	8530.9767338
38	9926.4611296	10059.3062914	10193.9138375	10330.3067866	10468.5084523
39	12160.9148837	12328.6798601	12498.7383647	12671.1212737	12845.8598710
40	14898.1207325	15109.7971685	15324.4532351	15542.1302422	15762.8700617

i	22.75	22.80	22.85	22.90	22.95
Years					
1	1.0000000	1.0000000	1.0000000	1.0000000	1.0000000
2	2.2275000	2.2280000	2.2285000	2.2290000	2.2295000
3	3.7342563	3.7359840	3.7377123	3.7394410	3.7411703
4	5.5837995	5.5877884	5.5917795	5.5957730	5.5997688
5	7.8541139	7.8618041	7.8695011	7.8772050	7.8849158
6	10.6409249	10.6542954	10.6676821	10.6810849	10.6945039
7	14.0617353	14.0834748	14.1052475	14.1270534	14.1488926
8	18.2607800	18.2945070	18.3282965	18.3621486	18.3960634
9	23.4151075	23.4656546	23.5163123	23.5670807	23.6179600
10	29.7420445	29.8158239	29.8897897	29.9639421	30.0382818
11	37.5083596	37.6138318	37.7196066	37.8256849	37.9320675
12	47.0415114	47.1897854	47.3385367	47.4877667	47.6374770
13	58.7434552	58.9490565	59.1553923	59.3624653	59.5702780
14	73.1075913	73.3894413	73.6723995	73.9564699	74.2416567
15	90.7395683	91.1222340	91.5065427	91.8925015	92.2801170
16	112.3828201	112.8981033	113.4157878	113.9358843	114.4584038
17	138.9499117	139.6388709	140.3312953	141.0272018	141.7266075
18	171.5610166	172.4765334	173.3969962	174.3224310	175.2528639
19	211.5911479	212.8011830	214.0182099	215.2422677	216.4733962
20	260.7281340	262.3198528	263.9213708	265.5327470	267.1540406
21	321.0437845	323.1287792	325.2274041	327.3397461	329.4658929
22	395.0812454	397.8021409	400.5418659	403.3005480	406.0783153
23	485.9622288	489.5010290	493.0656823	496.6563735	500.2732887
24	597.5186358	602.1072636	606.7311907	611.3906830	616.0860084
25	734.4541255	740.3877197	746.3692677	752.3991494	758.4777474
26	902.5424390	910.1961198	917.9146454	925.6985546	933.5483904
27	1108.8708439	1118.7208351	1128.6581419	1138.6835236	1148.7977460
28	1362.1389609	1374.7891855	1387.5565273	1400.4420505	1413.4468287
29	1673.0255745	1689.2411197	1705.6131938	1722.1432801	1738.8328758
30	2054.6388927	2075.3880950	2096.3458086	2117.5140913	2138.8950208
31	2523.0692408	2549.5765807	2576.3608258	2603.4248182	2630.7714281
32	3098.0674931	3131.8800411	3166.0592745	3200.6091015	3235.5334709
33	3803.8778478	3846.9486905	3890.5038188	3934.5485858	3979.0884024
34	4670.2600581	4725.0529919	4780.4839414	4836.5602119	4893.2891908
35	5733.7442213	5803.3650741	5873.8245220	5945.1325004	6017.2990601
36	7039.1710317	7127.5323110	7216.9934253	7307.5678430	7399.2691944
37	8641.5824414	8753.6096779	8867.0764229	8982.0008791	9098.4014745
38	10608.5424468	10750.4326845	10894.2033856	11039.8790804	11187.4846129
39	13022.9858535	13202.5313365	13384.5288592	13569.0113898	13756.0123315
40	15986.7151352	16213.7084812	16443.8937035	16677.3149980	16914.0171616

i	23.00	23.05	23.10	23.15	23.20
Years					
1	1.0000000	1.0000000	1.0000000	1.0000000	1.0000000
2	2.2300000	2.2305000	2.2310000	2.2315000	2.2320000
3	3.7429000	3.7446303	3.7463610	3.7480923	3.7498240
4	5.6037670	5.6077675	5.6117704	5.6157756	5.6197832
5	7.8926334	7.9003579	7.9080894	7.9158277	7.9235729
6	10.7079391	10.7213904	10.7348580	10.7483418	10.7618418
7	14.1707651	14.1926709	14.2146102	14.2365829	14.2585891
8	18.4300411	18.4640816	18.4981851	18.5323518	18.5665817
9	23.6689505	23.7200524	23.7712659	23.8225913	23.8740287
10	30.1128091	30.1875245	30.2624283	30.3375211	30.4128033
11	38.0387552	38.1457489	38.2530493	38.3606573	38.4685737
12	47.7876689	47.9383440	48.0895037	48.2411494	48.3932828
13	59.7788328	59.9881323	60.1981790	60.4089755	60.6205244
14	74.5279643	74.8153967	75.1039584	75.3936534	75.6844861
15	92.6693961	93.0603457	93.4529727	93.8472841	94.2432868
16	114.9833572	115.5107554	116.0406094	116.5729304	117.1077294
17	142.4295293	143.1359845	143.8459902	144.5595638	145.2767226
18	176.1883211	177.1288289	178.0744140	179.0251028	179.9809223
19	217.7116349	218.9570240	220.2096036	221.4694141	222.7364962
20	268.7853109	270.4266180	272.0780220	273.7395835	275.4113633
21	331.6059325	333.7599535	335.9280451	338.1102971	340.3067996
22	408.8752969	411.6916228	414.5274235	417.3828308	420.2579772
23	503.9166152	507.5865418	511.2832584	515.0069562	518.7578279
24	620.8174367	625.5852397	630.3896910	635.2310665	640.1096439
25	764.6054472	770.7826374	777.0097097	783.2870584	789.6150813
26	941.4647000	949.4480354	957.4989526	965.6180125	973.8057802
27	1159.0015810	1169.2958075	1179.6812107	1190.1585823	1200.7287212
28	1426.5719447	1439.8184911	1453.1875703	1466.6802942	1480.2977845
29	1755.6834919	1772.6966533	1789.8738991	1807.2167823	1824.7268705
30	2160.4906951	2182.3032319	2204.3347697	2226.5874674	2249.0635044
31	2658.4035549	2686.3241269	2714.5361015	2743.0424660	2771.8462375
32	3270.8363726	3306.5218381	3342.5939410	3379.0567969	3415.9145646
33	4024.1287383	4069.6751218	4115.7331414	4162.3084454	4209.4067436
34	4950.6783481	5008.7352374	5067.4674970	5126.8828505	5186.9891081
35	6090.3343681	6164.2487097	6239.0524888	6314.7562304	6391.3705811
36	7492.1112728	7586.1080372	7681.2736138	7777.6222978	7875.1685560
37	9216.2968656	9335.7059398	9456.6478185	9579.1418597	9703.2076609
38	11337.0451446	11488.5861589	11642.1334646	11797.7132003	11955.3518383
39	13945.5655279	14137.7052686	14332.4662949	14529.8838061	14729.9934648
40	17154.0455993	17397.4463330	17644.2660091	17894.5519072	18148.3519486

i	23.25	23.30	23.35	23.40	23.45
Years					
1	1.0000000	1.0000000	1.0000000	1.0000000	1.0000000
2	2.2325000	2.2330000	2.2335000	2.2340000	2.2345000
3	3.7515563	3.7532890	3.7550223	3.7567560	3.7584903
4	5.6237931	5.6278053	5.6318199	5.6358369	5.6398562
5	7.9313250	7.9390840	7.9468499	7.9546227	7.9624025
6	10.7753580	10.7888905	10.8024394	10.8160045	10.8295859
7	14.2806288	14.3027020	14.3248089	14.3469495	14.3691238
8	18.6008750	18.6352316	18.6696518	18.7041357	18.7386833
9	23.9255784	23.9772406	24.0290155	24.0809034	24.1329045
10	30.4882754	30.5639376	30.6397907	30.7158348	30.7920706
11	38.5767994	38.6853351	38.7941818	38.9033402	39.0128112
12	48.5459052	48.6990182	48.8526232	49.0067218	49.1613154
13	60.8328282	61.0458894	61.2597108	61.4742947	61.6896439
14	75.9764607	76.2695817	76.5638532	76.8592797	77.1558654
15	94.6409879	95.0403942	95.4415129	95.8443511	96.2489158
16	117.6450175	118.1848061	118.7271062	119.2719293	119.8192866
17	145.9974841	146.7218659	147.4498855	148.1815607	148.9169093
18	180.9418992	181.9080606	182.8794338	183.8560459	184.8379245
19	224.0108907	225.2926388	226.5817816	227.8783607	229.1824178
20	277.0934228	278.7858236	280.4886276	282.2018971	283.9256948
21	342.5176437	344.7429205	346.9827221	349.2371410	351.5062702
22	423.1529958	426.0680210	429.0031877	431.9586320	434.9344906
23	522.5360673	526.3418699	530.1754320	534.0369519	537.9266286
24	645.0257030	649.9795255	654.9713954	660.0015986	665.0704231
25	795.9941789	802.4247550	808.9072162	815.4419727	822.0294373
26	982.0628255	990.3897229	998.7870512	1007.2553943	1015.7953403
27	1211.3924325	1222.1505283	1233.0038277	1243.9531565	1254.9993476
28	1494.0411730	1507.9116014	1521.9102215	1536.0381952	1550.2966946
29	1842.4057457	1860.2550045	1878.2762582	1896.4711328	1914.8412695
30	2271.7650816	2294.6944206	2317.8537645	2341.2453779	2364.8715472
31	2800.9504631	2830.3582206	2860.0726185	2890.0967963	2920.4339251
32	3453.1714458	3490.8316860	3528.8995749	3567.3794467	3606.2756805
33	4257.0338069	4305.1954688	4353.8976256	4403.1462372	4452.9473276
34	5247.7941670	5309.3060131	5371.5327212	5434.4824567	5498.1634759
35	6468.9063108	6547.3743141	6626.7856116	6707.1513516	6788.4828110
36	7973.9270281	8073.9125293	8175.1400520	8277.6247678	8381.3820301
37	9828.8650621	9956.1341486	10085.0352541	10215.5889635	10347.8161162
38	12115.0761891	12276.9134053	12440.8909859	12607.0367810	12775.3789955
39	14932.8314030	15138.4342287	15346.8390311	15558.0833877	15772.2053699
40	18405.7147042	18666.6894040	18931.3259449	19199.6749004	19471.7875291

i	23.50	23.55	23.60	23.65	23.70
Years					
1	1.0000000	1.0000000	1.0000000	1.0000000	1.0000000
2	2.2350000	2.2355000	2.2360000	2.2365000	2.2370000
3	3.7602250	3.7619603	3.7636960	3.7654323	3.7671690
4	5.6438779	5.6479019	5.6519283	5.6559570	5.6599881
5	7.9701892	7.9779828	7.9857833	7.9935908	8.0014052
6	10.8431836	10.8567977	10.8704282	10.8840750	10.8977383
7	14.3913318	14.4135736	14.4358492	14.4581588	14.4805022
8	18.7732948	18.8079702	18.8427097	18.8775133	18.9123813
9	24.1850190	24.2372472	24.2895891	24.3420452	24.3946156
10	30.8684985	30.9451189	31.0219322	31.0989389	31.1761395
11	39.1225956	39.2326943	39.3431082	39.4538380	39.5648846
12	49.3164056	49.4719939	49.6280817	49.7846706	49.9417622
13	61.9057609	62.1226484	62.3403090	62.5587453	62.7779599
14	77.4536148	77.7525321	78.0526219	78.3538885	78.6563364
15	96.6552142	97.0632534	97.4730407	97.8845831	98.2978881
16	120.3691896	120.9216496	121.4766783	122.0342871	122.5944875
17	149.6559491	150.3986981	151.1451744	151.8953959	152.6493811
18	185.8250971	186.8175915	187.8154355	188.8186571	189.8272844
19	230.4939950	231.8131343	233.1398783	234.4742695	235.8163508
20	285.6600838	287.4051275	289.1608896	290.9274342	292.7048260
21	353.7902035	356.0890350	358.4028595	360.7317724	363.0758697
22	437.9309013	440.9480027	443.9859343	447.0448366	450.1248508
23	541.8446631	545.7912573	549.7666148	553.7709404	557.8044405
24	670.1781589	675.3250984	680.5115359	685.7377678	691.0040929
25	828.6700263	835.3641591	842.1122584	848.9147499	855.7720629
26	1024.4074825	1033.0924186	1041.8507514	1050.6830883	1059.5900418
27	1266.1432409	1277.3856832	1288.7275287	1300.1696387	1311.7128817
28	1564.6869025	1579.2100116	1593.8672255	1608.6597582	1623.5888346
29	1933.3883245	1952.1139693	1971.0198907	1990.1077911	2009.3793884
30	2388.7345808	2412.8368091	2437.1805849	2461.7682836	2486.6023035
31	2951.0872073	2982.0598776	3013.3552029	3044.9764827	3076.9270494
32	3645.5927010	3685.3349788	3725.5070308	3766.1134209	3807.1587602
33	4503.3069857	4554.2313663	4605.7266901	4657.7992449	4710.4553863
34	5562.5841274	5627.7528531	5693.6781890	5760.3687664	5827.8333129
35	6870.7913973	6954.0886500	7038.3862416	7123.6959796	7210.0298080
36	8486.4273757	8592.7765270	8700.4453946	8809.4500788	8919.8068725
37	10481.7378090	10617.3753992	10754.7505077	10893.8850224	11034.8011013
38	12945.9461941	13118.7673057	13293.8716275	13471.2888302	13651.0489623
39	15989.2435497	16209.2370061	16432.2253316	16658.2486386	16887.3475664
40	19747.7157839	20027.5123211	20311.2305098	20598.9244416	20890.6489397

i	23.75	23.80	23.85	23.90	23.95
Years					
1	1.0000000	1.0000000	1.0000000	1.0000000	1.0000000
2	2.2375000	2.2380000	2.2385000	2.2390000	2.2395000
3	3.7689063	3.7706440	3.7723823	3.7741210	3.7758603
4	5.6640215	5.6680573	5.6720954	5.6761359	5.6801788
5	8.0092266	8.0170549	8.0248902	8.0327324	8.0405816
6	10.9114179	10.9251140	10.9388265	10.9525554	10.9663009
7	14.5028797	14.5252911	14.5477366	14.5702162	14.5927300
8	18.9473136	18.9823104	19.0173718	19.0524979	19.0876888
9	24.4473005	24.5001002	24.5530149	24.6060449	24.6591902
10	31.2535344	31.3311241	31.4089090	31.4868896	31.5650663
11	39.6762488	39.7879316	39.8999338	40.0122562	40.1248997
12	50.0993579	50.2574594	50.4160680	50.5751854	50.7348132
13	62.9979555	63.2187347	63.4403002	63.6626547	63.8858009
14	78.9599699	79.2647936	79.5708118	79.8780292	80.1864502
15	98.7129627	99.1298144	99.5484505	99.9688782	100.3911051
16	123.1572914	123.7227103	124.2907559	124.8614401	125.4347747
17	153.4071481	154.1687153	154.9341012	155.7033243	156.4764033
18	190.8413458	191.8608695	192.8858843	193.9164188	194.9525018
19	237.1661654	238.5237565	239.8891677	241.2624429	242.6436260
20	294.4931296	296.2924105	298.1027342	299.9241667	301.7567745
21	365.4352479	367.8100042	370.2002363	372.6060426	375.0275219
22	453.2261193	456.3487852	459.4929927	462.6588868	465.8466134
23	561.8673227	565.9597961	570.0820715	574.2343607	578.4168774
24	696.3108118	701.6582276	707.0466455	712.4763729	717.9477195
25	862.6846296	869.6528858	876.6772705	883.7582261	890.8961983
26	1068.5722291	1077.6302726	1086.7647995	1095.9764421	1105.2658378
27	1323.3581335	1335.1062775	1346.9582042	1358.9148118	1370.9770059
28	1638.6556902	1653.8615715	1669.2077359	1684.6954518	1700.3259989
29	2028.8364167	2048.4806255	2068.3137809	2088.3376647	2108.5540756
30	2511.6850656	2537.0190144	2562.6066176	2588.4503666	2614.5527767
31	3109.2102687	3141.8295398	3174.7882959	3208.0900042	3241.7381667
32	3848.6477076	3890.5849703	3932.9753045	3975.8235152	4019.1344577
33	4763.7015381	4817.5441933	4871.9899146	4927.0453354	4982.7171603
34	5896.0806534	5965.1197113	6034.9595092	6105.6091705	6177.0779202
35	7297.3998086	7385.8182025	7475.2973521	7565.8497623	7657.4880820
36	9031.5322631	9144.6429347	9259.1557706	9375.0878555	9492.4564777
37	11177.5211756	11322.0679532	11468.4644219	11616.7338529	11766.8998041
38	13833.1824548	14017.7201261	14204.6931865	14394.1332437	14586.0723072
39	17119.5632879	17354.9375161	17593.5125115	17835.3310890	18080.4366247
40	21186.4595687	21486.4126449	21790.5652455	22098.9752193	22411.7011963

i	24.00	24.05	24.10	24.15	24.20
Years					
1	1.0000000	1.0000000	1.0000000	1.0000000	1.0000000
2	2.2400000	2.2405000	2.2410000	2.2415000	2.2420000
3	3.7776000	3.7793403	3.7810810	3.7828223	3.7845640
4	5.6842240	5.6882716	5.6923215	5.6963738	5.7004285
5	8.0484378	8.0563009	8.0641710	8.0720481	8.0799322
6	10.9800628	10.9938413	11.0076362	11.0214477	11.0352758
7	14.6152779	14.6378601	14.6604765	14.6831273	14.7058125
8	19.1229446	19.1582654	19.1936514	19.2291026	19.2646191
9	24.7124513	24.7658283	24.8193214	24.8729309	24.9266570
10	31.6434396	31.7220100	31.8007778	31.8797437	31.9589079
11	40.2378651	40.3511534	40.4647653	40.5787018	40.6929637
12	50.8949527	51.0556058	51.2167737	51.3784583	51.5406609
13	64.1097414	64.3344789	64.5600162	64.7863559	65.0135008
14	80.4960793	80.8069211	81.1189801	81.4322609	81.7467680
15	100.8151384	101.2409856	101.6686543	102.0981519	102.5294859
16	126.0107716	126.5894427	127.1708000	127.7548556	128.3416214
17	157.2533568	158.0342037	158.8189628	159.6076532	160.4002938
18	195.9941624	197.0414296	198.0943328	199.1529014	200.2171649
19	244.0327614	245.4298935	246.8350671	248.2483271	249.6697189
20	303.6006241	305.4557829	307.3223182	309.2002981	311.0897908
21	377.4647739	379.9178986	382.3869969	384.8721701	387.3735202
22	469.0563196	472.2881533	475.5422632	478.8187992	482.1179121
23	582.6298363	586.8734541	591.1479486	595.4535392	599.7904468
24	723.4609971	729.0165198	734.6146042	740.2555689	745.9397350
25	898.0916364	905.3449929	912.6567238	920.0272888	927.4571508
26	1114.6336291	1124.0804636	1133.6069943	1143.2138790	1152.9017813
27	1383.1457001	1395.4218151	1407.8062799	1420.3000308	1432.9040124
28	1716.1006681	1732.0207617	1748.0875933	1764.3024883	1780.6667834
29	2128.9648284	2149.5717549	2170.3767033	2191.3815392	2212.5881450
30	2640.9163873	2667.5437619	2694.4374888	2721.6001809	2749.0344761
31	3275.7363202	3310.0880366	3344.7969236	3379.8666246	3415.3008193
32	4062.9130370	4107.1642094	4151.8929822	4197.1044144	4242.8036176
33	5039.0121659	5095.9372018	5153.4991909	5211.7051305	5270.5620931
34	6249.3750858	6322.5100989	6396.4924959	6471.3319195	6547.0381196
35	7750.2251063	7844.0737776	7939.0471874	8035.1585781	8132.4213445
36	9611.2791319	9731.5735212	9853.3575596	9976.6493747	10101.4673099
37	11918.9861235	12073.0169530	12229.0167315	12387.0101987	12547.0223989
38	14780.5427932	14977.5775302	15177.2097638	15379.4731617	15584.4018194
39	18328.8730635	18580.6849262	18835.9173168	19094.6159303	19356.8270597
40	22728.8025988	23050.3396509	23376.3733902	23706.9656774	24042.1792082

i	24.25	24.30	24.35	24.40	24.45
Years					
1	1.0000000	1.0000000	1.0000000	1.0000000	1.0000000
2	2.2425000	2.2430000	2.2435000	2.2440000	2.2445000
3	3.7863063	3.7880490	3.7897923	3.7915360	3.7932803
4	5.7044855	5.7085449	5.7126067	5.7166708	5.7207373
5	8.0878233	8.0957213	8.1036264	8.1115385	8.1194575
6	11.0491204	11.0629816	11.0768594	11.0907538	11.1046649
7	14.7285321	14.7512861	14.7740747	14.7968978	14.8197555
8	19.3002011	19.3358487	19.3715619	19.4073408	19.4431857
9	24.9804999	25.0344599	25.0885372	25.1427320	25.1970446
10	32.0382711	32.1178336	32.1975960	32.2775586	32.3577220
11	40.8075519	40.9224672	41.0377106	41.1532829	41.2691850
12	51.7033832	51.8666267	52.0303931	52.1946839	52.3595007
13	65.2414536	65.4702170	65.6997939	65.9301868	66.1613987
14	82.0625061	82.3794798	82.6976937	83.0171524	83.3378606
15	102.9626638	103.3976934	103.8345821	104.2733376	104.7139676
16	128.9311098	129.5233328	130.1183028	130.7160319	131.3165326
17	161.1969039	161.9975027	162.8021095	163.6107437	164.4234249
18	201.2871531	202.3628959	203.4444232	204.5317652	205.6249523
19	251.0992878	252.5370796	253.9831402	255.4375159	256.9002531
20	312.9908651	314.9035899	316.8280349	318.7642698	320.7123650
21	389.8911499	392.4251623	394.9756614	397.5427516	400.1265382
22	485.4397537	488.7844767	492.1522349	495.5431830	498.9574768
23	604.1588940	608.5591046	612.9913041	617.4557197	621.9525799
24	751.6674258	757.4389670	763.2546867	769.1149153	775.0199856
25	934.9467765	942.4966359	950.1072029	957.7789546	965.5123721
26	1162.6713698	1172.5233185	1182.4583068	1192.4770195	1202.5801471
27	1445.6191770	1458.4464849	1471.3869045	1484.4414123	1497.6109931
28	1797.1818274	1813.8489807	1830.6696157	1847.6451169	1864.7768809
29	2233.9984206	2255.6142830	2277.4376671	2299.4705254	2321.7148282
30	2776.7430375	2804.7285538	2832.9937391	2861.5413336	2890.3741037
31	3451.1032241	3487.2775923	3523.8277145	3560.7574190	3598.0705721
32	4288.9957560	4335.6860473	4382.8797630	4430.5822292	4478.7988270
33	5330.0772268	5390.2577568	5451.1109853	5512.6442932	5574.8651402
34	6623.6209543	6701.0903917	6779.4565102	6858.7295007	6938.9196669
35	8230.8490358	8330.4553568	8431.2541705	8533.2594989	8636.4855255
36	10227.8299269	10355.7560085	10485.2645610	10616.3748166	10749.1062365
37	12709.0786842	12873.2047186	13039.4264816	13207.7702719	13378.2627113
38	15792.0302651	16002.3934652	16215.5268298	16431.4662182	16650.2479442
39	19622.5976044	19891.9750773	20165.0076129	20441.7439754	20722.2335666
40	24382.0775235	24726.7250211	25076.1869667	25430.5295054	25789.8196736

i	24.50	24.55	24.60	24.65	24.70
Years					
1	1.0000000	1.0000000	1.0000000	1.0000000	1.0000000
2	2.2450000	2.2455000	2.2460000	2.2465000	2.2470000
3	3.7950250	3.7967703	3.7985160	3.8002623	3.8020090
4	5.7248061	5.7288773	5.7329509	5.7370269	5.7411052
5	8.1273836	8.1353167	8.1432569	8.1512040	8.1591582
6	11.1185926	11.1325370	11.1464981	11.1604758	11.1744703
7	14.8426478	14.8655748	14.8885366	14.9115331	14.9345645
8	19.4790965	19.5150734	19.5511166	19.5872260	19.6234019
9	25.2514752	25.3060240	25.3606913	25.4154772	25.4703821
10	32.4380866	32.5186529	32.5994213	32.6803924	32.7615665
11	41.3854178	41.5019821	41.6188789	41.7361091	41.8536735
12	52.5248451	52.6907188	52.8571232	53.0240600	53.1915308
13	66.3934322	66.6262902	66.8599755	67.0944908	67.3298389
14	83.6598231	83.9830445	84.3075294	84.6332827	84.9603091
15	105.1564798	105.6008819	106.0471817	106.4953869	106.9455055
16	131.9198173	132.5258984	133.1347883	133.7464998	134.3610453
17	165.2401725	166.0610064	166.8859463	167.7150120	168.5482235
18	206.7240148	207.8289835	208.9398891	210.0567624	211.1796347
19	258.3713984	259.8509989	261.3391018	262.8357544	264.3410045
20	322.6723911	324.6444192	326.6285208	328.6247678	330.6332326
21	402.7271269	405.3446241	407.9791369	410.6307731	413.2996411
22	502.3952730	505.8567293	509.3420046	512.8512587	516.3846524
23	626.4821148	631.0445563	635.6401377	640.2690940	644.9316616
24	780.9702330	786.9659949	793.0076116	799.0954256	805.2297820
25	973.3079400	981.1661467	989.0874841	997.0724480	1005.1215381
26	1212.7683853	1223.0424357	1233.4030052	1243.8508065	1254.3865580
27	1510.8966397	1524.2993536	1537.8201444	1551.4600303	1565.2200378
28	1882.0663165	1899.5148450	1917.1239000	1934.8949277	1952.8293872
29	2344.1725640	2366.8457394	2389.7363794	2412.8465274	2436.1782458
30	2919.4948422	2948.9063684	2978.6115287	3008.6131964	3038.9142725
31	3635.7710785	3673.8628819	3712.3499647	3751.2363494	3790.5260978
32	4527.5349928	4576.7962194	4626.5880561	4676.9161095	4727.7860440
33	5637.7810660	5701.3996912	5765.7287179	5830.7759305	5896.5491969
34	7020.0374272	7102.0933154	7185.0979824	7269.0621973	7353.9968485
35	8740.9465968	8846.6572243	8953.6320861	9061.8860290	9171.4340701
36	10883.4785131	11019.5115729	11157.2255793	11296.6409351	11437.7782854
37	13550.9307488	13725.8016641	13902.9030718	14082.2629256	14263.9095219
38	16871.9087822	17096.4859726	17324.0172275	17554.5407368	17788.0951738
39	21006.5264339	21294.6732789	21586.7254655	21882.7350284	22182.7546817
40	26154.1254102	26523.5155688	26898.0599300	27277.8292129	27662.8950881

i	24.75	24.80	24.85	24.90	24.95
Years					
1	1.0000000	1.0000000	1.0000000	1.0000000	1.0000000
2	2.2475000	2.2480000	2.2485000	2.2490000	2.2495000
3	3.8037563	3.8055040	3.8072523	3.8090010	3.8107503
4	5.7451859	5.7492690	5.7533544	5.7574422	5.7615324
5	8.1671194	8.1750877	8.1830630	8.1910454	8.1990348
6	11.1884815	11.2025095	11.2165542	11.2306157	11.2446940
7	14.9576307	14.9807318	15.0038679	15.0270390	15.0502451
8	19.6596443	19.6959533	19.7323290	19.7687717	19.8052813
9	25.5254062	25.5805497	25.6358128	25.6911958	25.7466989
10	32.8429443	32.9245260	33.0063123	33.0883036	33.1705003
11	41.9715730	42.0898085	42.2083809	42.3272912	42.4465401
12	53.3595373	53.5280810	53.6971636	53.8667867	54.0369519
13	67.5660227	67.8030451	68.0409087	68.2796165	68.5191714
14	85.2886134	85.6182002	85.9490745	86.2812411	86.6147047
15	107.3975452	107.8515139	108.3074195	108.7652701	109.2250735
16	134.9784376	135.5986893	136.2218133	136.8478223	137.4767293
17	169.3856009	170.2271643	171.0729339	171.9229301	172.7771733
18	212.3085371	213.4435010	214.5845580	215.7317397	216.8850780
19	265.8549001	267.3774893	268.9088206	270.4489429	271.9979050
20	332.6539878	334.6871066	336.7326626	338.7907296	340.8613822
21	415.9858498	418.6895091	421.4107292	424.1496213	426.9062971
22	519.9423476	523.5245073	527.1312954	530.7628770	534.4194182
23	649.6280787	654.3585851	659.1234224	663.9228334	668.7570631
24	811.4110281	817.6395142	823.9155928	830.2396189	836.6119503
25	1013.2352576	1021.4141138	1029.6586176	1037.9692841	1046.3466320
26	1265.0109839	1275.7248140	1286.5287841	1297.4236358	1308.4101166
27	1579.1012024	1593.1045679	1607.2311869	1621.4821211	1635.8584407
28	1970.9287500	1989.1945007	2007.6281369	2026.2311693	2045.0051217
29	2459.7336156	2483.5147369	2507.5237289	2531.7627304	2556.2338996
30	3069.5176855	3100.4263916	3131.6433756	3163.1716503	3195.0142575
31	3830.2233126	3870.3321367	3910.8567544	3951.8013912	3993.1703147
32	4779.2035825	4831.1745066	4883.7046578	4936.7999376	4990.4663083
33	5963.0564691	6030.3057843	6098.3052653	6167.0631221	6236.5876522
34	7439.9129452	7526.8216188	7614.7341237	7703.6618395	7793.6162714
35	9282.2913992	9394.4733802	9507.9955535	9622.8736375	9739.1235311
36	11580.6585205	11725.3027785	11871.7324485	12019.9691733	12170.0348521
37	14447.8715043	14634.1778676	14822.8579620	15013.9414974	15207.4585477
38	18024.7197016	18264.4539788	18507.3381656	18753.4129303	19002.7194554
39	22486.8378278	22795.0385655	23107.4116997	23424.0127499	23744.8979595
40	28053.3301901	28449.2081297	28850.6035071	29257.5919246	29670.2500004

i	25.00	25.05	25.10	25.15	25.20
Years					
1	1.0000000	1.0000000	1.0000000	1.0000000	1.0000000
2	2.2500000	2.2505000	2.2510000	2.2515000	2.2520000
3	3.8125000	3.8142503	3.8160010	3.8177523	3.8195040
4	5.7656250	5.7697199	5.7738173	5.7779169	5.7820190
5	8.2070313	8.2150348	8.2230454	8.2310631	8.2390878
6	11.2587891	11.2729010	11.2870298	11.3011754	11.3153379
7	15.0734863	15.0967627	15.1200742	15.1434210	15.1668031
8	19.8418579	19.8785017	19.9152129	19.9519914	19.9888375
9	25.8023224	25.8580664	25.9139313	25.9699173	26.0260245
10	33.2529030	33.3355121	33.4183281	33.5013514	33.5845827
11	42.5661287	42.6860579	42.8063284	42.9269413	43.0478975
12	54.2076609	54.3789153	54.5507169	54.7230671	54.8959677
13	68.7595761	69.0008336	69.2429468	69.4859184	69.7297515
14	86.9494702	87.2855425	87.6229264	87.9616269	88.3016489
15	109.6868377	110.1505709	110.6162810	111.0839761	111.5536644
16	138.1085472	138.7432889	139.3809675	140.0215961	140.6651879
17	173.6356839	174.4984827	175.3655903	176.2370275	177.1128152
18	218.0446049	219.2103526	220.3823535	221.5606399	222.7452446
19	273.5557562	275.1225460	276.6983242	278.2831409	279.8770463
20	342.9446952	345.0407437	347.1496036	349.2713508	351.4060620
21	429.6808690	432.4734501	435.2841541	438.1130955	440.9603896
22	538.1010862	541.8080493	545.5404767	549.2985390	553.0824077
23	673.6263578	678.5309656	683.4711364	688.4471216	693.4591745
24	843.0329473	849.5029725	856.0223916	862.5915727	869.2108865
25	1054.7911841	1063.3034671	1071.8840119	1080.5333532	1089.2520299
26	1319.4889801	1330.6609857	1341.9268989	1353.2874916	1364.7435414
27	1650.3612251	1664.9915626	1679.7505506	1694.6392957	1709.6589138
28	2063.9515314	2083.0719490	2102.3679388	2121.8410786	2141.4929601
29	2580.9394142	2605.8814722	2631.0622914	2656.4841098	2682.1491860
30	3227.1742678	3259.6547810	3292.4589266	3325.5898635	3359.0507809
31	4034.9678347	4077.1983037	4119.8661171	4162.9757141	4206.5315777
32	5044.7097934	5099.5364787	5154.9525125	5210.9641062	5267.5775353
33	6306.8872418	6377.9703667	6449.8455932	6522.5215789	6596.0070741
34	7884.6090522	7976.6519435	8069.7568370	8163.9357560	8259.2008568
35	9856.7613153	9975.8032554	10096.2658031	10218.1655987	10341.5194727
36	12321.9516441	12475.7419708	12631.4285197	12789.0342468	12948.5823799
37	15403.4395551	15601.9153345	15802.9170782	16006.4763598	16212.6251396
38	19255.2994439	19511.1951258	19770.4492648	20033.1051643	20299.2066748
39	24070.1243048	24399.7495049	24733.8320302	25072.4311131	25415.6067568
40	30088.6553811	30512.8867558	30943.0238698	31379.1475381	31821.3396595

Lightning Source UK Ltd.
Milton Keynes UK
UKHW020638240521
384271UK00011B/908

9 783753 436166